Letters from Jesus

Jake Provance

WORD & SPIRIT
PUBLISHING

Letters from Jesus
ISBN: 978-1-685730-41-3
Copyright © 2023 by Word and Spirit Publishing

Published by Word and Spirit Publishing
P.O. Box 701403
Tulsa, Oklahoma 74170
wordandspiritpublishing.com

Contents

Preface

Letter from the Author:

In both the Old and New Testaments, Jesus' presence is evident on every page. While Jesus made His physical debut in the New Testament, His influence was not absent in the unfolding story of God and humanity. This book is written from a personable perspective, embodying the voice of Christ, so readers can truly feel and understand His presence speaking through each word of the Bible. Every letter is crafted with reverence and honor, representing Christ's voice in a personal manner, yet deeply rooted in Scripture. In a grand finale, the book culminates with a retelling of the story of God and humanity, from Genesis to Revelation, through the eyes of Jesus. The aim of this book is to serve as a vessel through which the Lord can foster an intimate relationship with His children, igniting a fervent passion for God, His Word, and His Ways. This book is chock-full of the Bible; every word is rooted in biblical principles and faith. I do not intend to compare the importance of this book with that of the Bible. This book is created out of profound respect and admiration for God's written Word. It is intended as a tool to direct people to the Bible, for the Bible is the divinely inspired Word of God. Every word, both in the Old and New Testaments, is for our benefit today. His Word is above contestation. It is immune to corruption. It is the lamp that lights the path for every believer. It is the gate through which faith is welcomed and doubt is shut out. It is the bread of life—living, active, and sharp. It separates all things into their proper places with perfect discernment. As we read it, pray it, speak it, think it, obey it, and enjoy it, we undergo a metamorphosis from who we were to who we are in Christ. In it, we are new creatures in Christ, full of freedom and strength. We are overcomers and more than conquerors. We are children of the one true God—chosen, redeemed, righteous, protected, and loved. It is the pearl of great price, worth more than we have to give, and yet we are called to utilize it as an ambassador for His Kingdom, and a temple for His Holy Spirit. Through it, we have gained authority and dominion, wisdom and guidance, provision and victory, a peace that passes understanding, a joy that surpasses explanation, and a hope that never fades. Not a single word is unfruitful. Every word is watched over by the Father. He is ever searching for someone who will take Him at His Word. May God use this book as a tool to draw you close and ignite a passion inside of you for Him.

May you be that somebody who takes Him at His Word.

Christ's ambassador,
Jake Provance

He Would Be Born of a Virgin

Prophecy:

Therefore the Lord himself will give you a sign. Behold, the virgin shall conceive and bear a son, and shall call his name Immanuel.

– Isaiah 7:14 ESV

Fulfilled:

All this took place to fulfill what the Lord had spoken by the prophet: "Behold, the virgin shall conceive and bear a son, and they shall call his name Immanuel" (which means, God with us).

– Matthew 1:22–23 ESV

1

Hope

My Dear Friend,

I am the Source of hope. I am the One who brings light to the darkness, who gives you the strength to keep going even when things seem impossible. I am the One who will never leave you nor forsake you, and I am the One who promises to guide you and give you the peace that surpasses all understanding.

I know at times you may feel hopeless and lost. You may face challenges and difficulties that seem insurmountable, and they may tempt you to despair. Don't give in to that temptation. No matter what you face, remember—there is always hope. Never think for one second that I don't have the ability or the will to put you over and above in any situation.

Hope is not about what you see in the present; it is about what you know to be true in the future. It is a confident expectation born in the heart of faith. You can expect a good outcome because you have more faith in My ability to help you than in this world's ability to harm you. You expect a bright future because you trust more in My love for you than in your enemies' hatred of you.

I recall a story of when My disciples woke Me in the midst of a storm while I was belowdecks sleeping. So, I arose and quieted the wind and the waves. Faith is what quieted the wind and the waves that day. It was love that caused Me to quiet the storm and remind My disciples that there was no need for fear while I was with them. As for hope: Hope was the reason I was asleep during the storm in the first place.

Hope, then, becomes an anchor for your soul. It provides stability and solid footing wherever your feet may tread. It offers uncommon confidence, a sincere smile, and a peace that doesn't make sense in the middle of the terrible storm. Trust in Me. Hope in Me. Fix your eyes on Me instead of on the troubles that surround you. Have I not said, and will I not make it so? Refuse to doubt. Refuse to give in to despair. Trust in what I said more than what your situation says.

Hold on to hope. Hold on to Me.

With all My love,

Jesus

(Titus 2:13; John 1:5; Matthew 4:16; 1 Peter 1:3; Romans 12:12; Isaiah 40:29; Isaiah 40:31; Romans 8:24–25; 2 Corinthians 4:18; Psalm 34:19; Mark 4:25–41; Hebrews 6:19–20; Philippians 4:6–7; Hebrews 12:1–2; Isaiah 46:11; Proverbs 23:18)

Scriptures on Hope

May the God of your hope so fill you with all joy and peace in believing [through the experience of your faith] that by the power of the Holy Spirit you may abound *and* be overflowing (bubbling over) with hope.

– ROMANS 15:13 AMPC

Rejoice and exult in hope; be steadfast and patient in suffering and tribulation; be constant in prayer.

– ROMANS 12:12 AMPC

[Now] we have this [hope] as a sure and steadfast anchor of the soul [it cannot slip and it cannot break down under whoever steps out upon it—a hope] that reaches farther and enters into [the very certainty of the Presence] within the veil.

– HEBREWS 6:19 AMPC

Be of good courage, and He shall strengthen your heart, all you who hope in the LORD.

– PSALM 31:24 NKJV

But those who hope in the LORD will renew their strength. They will soar on wings like eagles; they will run and not grow weary, they will walk and not be faint.

– ISAIAH 40:31 NIV

Yet I still dare to hope when I remember this: The faithful love of the LORD never ends! His mercies never cease. Great is his faithfulness; his mercies begin afresh each morning.

– LAMENTATIONS 3:21–23 NLT

And now abide faith, hope, love, these three; but the greatest of these is love.

– 1 CORINTHIANS 13:13 NKJV

The Price for His Betrayal Would Be Thirty Pieces of Silver

Prophecy:

And I said to them, "If it is good in your sight, give me my wages; but if not, never mind!" So they weighed out thirty shekels of silver as my wages.

– Zechariah 11:12 NASB1995

Fulfilled:

Then one of the twelve, named Judas Iscariot, went to the chief priests and said, "What are you willing to give me to betray Him to you?" And they weighed out thirty pieces of silver to him.

– Matthew 26:14–15 NASB1995

2

Faith

Dearest Child,

I come to you today to speak of a topic that is near and dear to My heart: faith. Faith is the foundation upon which all things are built. It was faith that created you, as well as the world in which you live. Faith opens the way for hope in your heart. Faith gives proof to the unseen realm. Through faith you have received eternal life.

Faith is not just a concept or an idea; it is a living, breathing, eternal force that has the power to change your life. It is the very essence of who I am and what I stand for. I am the embodiment of faith. Faith comes when you hear My Word. Through reading, listening, and studying Me and My words, the seed of faith inside you begins to take root and eventually grow.

You see, My Father placed inside you a seed of faith the moment you received Me as your Savior. The same faith that created the world, that brought Me back to life, that saved your soul—a measure of that same faith lives in you. Now it is your charge to value that seed. Like any seed, it must be nurtured and tended to for it to take root, grow, and flourish.

You know how faith comes—by hearing the Word. After that, the task becomes how to make it stay and take root in your life. You must act on it! Faith is an act. Faith without works is dead. It is not enough to simply believe, but you must follow up that belief with action. You'll never see the joyous fruit of faith if you only hear what I'm saying but never do what I'm telling you to do.

If you haven't noticed, this world brings with it many problems that will put the heat and pressure on you and your faith. Remember to be cheerful and choose to rejoice anyway. Why? Because I have already overcome the world, and all these tests and trials are really doing is refining your faith!

Finally, know this: Even if your faith fails, I won't. If you begin to sink, I'll catch you. If you become afflicted, I'll deliver you. Even if you begin to doubt, I'll still come to you. There is always a better way, a more blessed way, a way of victory that I wish for you. It is the way of faith. But I won't leave you if you stumble off the path. I'll rescue you and then show you the way back to the path.

Triumphantly yours,

Jesus

(Hebrews 11; Matthew 7:24–25; 1 Peter 1:7; James 1:2–3; Ephesians 2:8–9; Romans 10:17; Romans 12:3; James 2:14–17; Matthew 14:22–33; Mark 9:23–24)

Scriptures on Faith ────────────────

Now faith is the assurance (the confirmation, the title deed) of the things [we] hope for, being the proof of things [we] do not see and the conviction of their reality [faith perceiving as real fact what is not revealed to the senses]. For by [faith—trust and holy fervor born of faith] the men of old had divine testimony borne to them and obtained a good report. By faith we understand that the worlds [during the successive ages were framed (fashioned, put in order, and equipped for their intended purpose) by the word of God, so that what we see was not made out of things which are visible].

– HEBREWS 11:1–3 AMPC

For by grace are ye saved through faith; and that not of yourselves: it is the gift of God.

– EPHESIANS 2:8 KJV

Jesus replied, "Truly I tell you, if you have faith and do not doubt, not only can you do what was done to the fig tree, but also you can say to this mountain, 'Go, throw yourself into the sea,' and it will be done."

– MATTHEW 21:21 NIV

And it is impossible to please God without faith. Anyone who wants to come to him must believe that God exists and that he rewards those who sincerely seek him.

– HEBREWS 11:6 NLT

Be alert and on your guard; stand firm in your faith (your conviction respecting man's relationship to God and divine things, keeping the trust and holy fervor born of faith and a part of it). Act like men and be courageous; grow in strength!

– 1 CORINTHIANS 16:13 AMPC

He Would Die Amongst Criminals

Prophecy:

Therefore I will give him a portion among the great, and he will divide the spoils with the strong, because he poured out his life unto death, and was numbered with the transgressors. For he bore the sin of many, and made intercession for the transgressors.

— Isaiah 53:12 NIV

Fulfilled:

They crucified two robbers with Him, one on His right and one on His left.

— Mark 15:27 NASB1995

3

Love

My Beloved,

I love you. I laid aside My power and glory in heaven to become like every other person, not out of duty or obligation, but out of love. I wanted you to have the same close, intimate, and personal relationship with God the Father that I have.

You see, God is love. So, every time I spoke in My Word to you and told of how I was doing the will of My Father, I was also saying that I was doing Love's will. All My actions on the earth—every healing, every word spoken, every miracle performed—were motivated by and for love.

In the Garden of Gethsemane, I began to sweat blood. My body was under extreme stress and pressure because I knew the horror that awaited Me. It would be the first and only time in all time and eternity that I would ever be separated from My Father. I also knew that if I were never separated from Him, taking your place on the cross, then you could never take My place being reconnected to Him and adopted into His family.

Still, as I prayed to the Father, I knew how loving, infinitely intelligent, and wise He is. If there was another way you could have received salvation without Me being separated from Him, then He would have known it and done it, regardless of how difficult it might have been, because of His great love and desire not to be separated from Me. So, I asked Him for just that, knowing that if this was the only way, I was willing to do it—for you and for Him.

You see, My beloved, it was not the might of the people or any army that captured Me and put Me in shackles; it was love. It was not the authority of Pilate to whom I submitted, but the authority of love. It was not the will of men to which I yielded, but the will of love. With every lash I received, I thought of you. I thought of the pain and torment that was caused by sin and sickness. It wasn't the nails that kept me on the cross; it was love. So, I stayed, and I bore it, because of you—because of love.

Do not go another day, My beloved, My dearest friend, thinking for one moment that My love for you is ever in question. There is nothing and no one in all time and eternity—angelic or demonic, known or unknown—that can separate you from the love of our Father shown by Me on the earth. Our love for you is unconditional. You didn't earn it, so you can't lose it.

So, from heaven to you: We love you.

Forever yours,

Jesus

(Philippians 2:5–8; John 14:6–7; John 15:15; 1 John 4:8; John 6:38; Matthew 26:38–39; Luke 22:44; Matthew 27:46; John 1:12–13; Galatians 4:4–5; John 18:4–6; John 19:10–11; Isaiah 53:4–5; Romans 8:38–39; John 15:13; 1 John 4:19)

Scriptures on Love————————————————

Love endures long and is patient and kind; love never is envious nor boils over with jealousy, is not boastful or vainglorious, does not display itself haughtily. It is not conceited (arrogant and inflated with pride); it is not rude (unmannerly) and does not act unbecomingly. Love (God's love in us) does not insist on its own rights or its own way, for it is not self-seeking; it is not touchy or fretful or resentful; it takes no account of the evil done to it, [it pays no attention to a suffered wrong]. It does not rejoice at injustice and unrighteousness, but rejoices when right and truth prevail. Love bears up under anything and everything that comes, is ever ready to believe the best of every person, its hopes are fadeless under all circumstances, and it endures everything [without weakening]. Love never fails [never fades out or becomes obsolete or comes to an end].

                                          – 1 CORINTHIANS 13:4–8 AMPC

Though I speak with the tongues of men and of angels, but have not love, I have become sounding brass or a clanging cymbal. And though I have the gift of prophecy, and understand all mysteries and all knowledge, and though I have all faith, so that I could remove mountains, but have not love, I am nothing. And though I bestow all my goods to feed the poor, and though I give my body to be burned, but have not love, it profits me nothing.

                                          – 1 CORINTHIANS 13:1–3 NKJV

And above all things have fervent love for one another, for "love will cover a multitude of sins."

                                          – 1 PETER 4:8 NKJV

Let all that you do be done with love.

                                          – 1 CORINTHIANS 16:14 NKJV

And we have known and believed the love that God has for us. God is love, and he who abides in love abides in God, and God in him.

                                          – 1 JOHN 4:16 NKJV

He Would Be Born in Bethlehem

Prophecy:

But you, Bethlehem Ephrathah, though you are small among the clans of Judah, out of you will come for me one who will be ruler over Israel, whose origins are from of old, from ancient times.

— MICAH 5:2 NIV

Fulfilled:

After Jesus was born in Bethlehem in Judea, during the time of King Herod, Magi from the east came to Jerusalem.

— MATTHEW 2:1 NIV

4

Guidance

My Dear Friend,

I am the Good Shepherd, which means I am *your* Good Shepherd. I am not some far-off, aloof Shepherd who is unaware of the state of His flock. No, I tend to you, I know where you are, and I will lead you where you need to go. The path I have set before you is not one that is fraught with mayhem and difficulty. With me as your Shepherd, you can expect a light and easy load. I won't lean on you, ask you to do something too difficult for you to handle, or lead you to a place where you are ill-equipped to go. I will lead you beside the still waters and the green fields, My precious one.

Will you follow Me?

I can lead the way, even light up the path through My Word. I can rescue you again and again when you wander off, but I can't, *and I won't*, force you to follow Me. Often, people will come to Me seeking guidance on a decision, but they don't seek for My guidance throughout their lives. They want to go their own way, and they want My help to get where *they* want to go.

They don't value My things or My way. If you are to seek My guidance, you must seek My way. When you seek and structure your life in pursuit of My way of doing things, getting to know Me through reading My Word and spending time with Me in prayer, intimately and fervently acknowledging Me, then I will direct your path.

The decision that may be burning of urgency in front of you may not be what I want to talk to you about. Are you willing to listen to Me? The problems before you may not be caused by what you think. Are you willing to trust Me?

My guidance is gentle; it's a whisper, a nudge, and a sense of peace. It requires closeness and intimacy. Many have searched for Me in the loud, noisy things of the world, the powerful and forceful happenings. But those who know Me know to look for the subtle, gentle whisper. I write to you this day to encourage you to come away with Me. Rest in Me, and take refuge in Me, away from all the troubles of the world. Let us talk privately, you and Me. Let Me show you My ways in My Word. Instead of seeking an answer, seek Me.

I love you. I'm looking forward to spending time with you very soon.

Jesus

(John 10:11–15; Matthew 11:28–30; Proverbs 6:23; Psalm 119:105; Psalm 23; John 15:5; Joshua 1:8; 1 Kings 19:12; Romans 8:28; Proverbs 3:5–6; James 1:5; Philippians 4:6–7; Psalm 32:8; John 10:14; Matthew 6:6)

Scriptures on Guidance ————————————————

Lead me in thy truth, and teach me: for thou art the God of my salvation; on thee do I wait all the day.

— PSALM 25:5 KJV

I will instruct thee and teach thee in the way which thou shalt go: I will guide thee with mine eye.

— PSALM 32:8 KJV

Trust in the LORD with all thine heart; and lean not unto thine own understanding. In all thy ways acknowledge him, and he shall direct thy paths.

— PROVERBS 3:5–6 KJV

And thine ears shall hear a word behind thee, saying, This is the way, walk ye in it, when ye turn to the right hand, and when ye turn to the left.

— ISAIAH 30:21 KJV

Howbeit when he, the Spirit of truth, is come, he will guide you into all truth: for he shall not speak of himself; but whatsoever he shall hear, that shall he speak: and he will shew you things to come.

— JOHN 16:13 KJV

If any of you lack wisdom, let him ask of God, that giveth to all men liberally, and upbraideth not; and it shall be given him.

— JAMES 1:5 KJV

He Would Be Called Out from Egypt

Prophecy:

When Israel was a child, I loved him, and out of Egypt I called my son.

– HOSEA 11:1 NIV

Fulfilled:

So he got up, took the child and his mother during the night and left for Egypt, where he stayed until the death of Herod. And so was fulfilled what the Lord had said through the prophet: "Out of Egypt I called my son."

– MATTHEW 2:14–15 NIV

5

Grace and Mercy

Dearest Child,

I come to you today with a message of mercy. For too long, you have been burdened by guilt, shame, and fear, thinking you are not worthy of My love and forgiveness. But I tell you, My child, that My mercy is boundless, and it is available to all who seek it.

I also come to you with the glad tidings of grace. Through the gift of grace, you can live boldly and come to Me confidently. It is by the gift of grace that you have received salvation. It is through My grace that you have the right to come to the throne boldly to obtain mercy when your need is dire.

I am your High Priest, and I know what it is like to walk a day in your shoes. I am not unable to sympathize or have shared feelings concerning your situation. Yet I, because I did not sin, can stand in the gap, connecting you to the Father.

My friend, when the situation in which you find yourself is horrible and you can't even blame the devil for the sorry state of affairs because of how bad you messed up, the Father's mercy can wash it away in a moment if you but ask Him. Who is it that can hold you answerable for a sin when He's forgiven it? Who can lay a charge against the one whom He has acquitted? Whose throne sits above His? I tell you the truth, there is none. Don't believe for a second that anything you have done is more powerful than what I have done for you at the cross.

It is important to understand that mercy and grace are closely related, but they are not the same thing. Mercy is shown when I choose not to punish you for your sins, but grace is shown when I give you what you don't deserve, which is salvation and forgiveness.

Neither mercy nor grace can be earned, which means neither can be lost through your mistakes. Both mercy and grace are always available to anyone who would believe and ask for them. So, come and ask. Receive the help you need. Live freely in the light. Let Me take the burdens off your shoulders. Cast your cares on Me because I care for you.

Then, in your free state provided by mercy and grace, I call upon you to share these gifts with others. Be merciful as I am merciful. Forgive as I have forgiven. Show compassion as I have shown compassion to you. And in doing so, you will reflect My love to the world.

Grace and peace,

Jesus

(Ephesians 2:8–9; Romans 3:23–24; Hebrews 4:14–16; Hebrews 7:25; Ezekiel 22:30; Isaiah 55:7; 1 Timothy 2:5; 1 John 1:9; Ephesians 2:4–5; Psalm 103:8–10; Matthew 11:28–30; Luke 6:36; 2 Corinthians 12:9; Romans 5:8; Psalm 103:17; Psalm 136:1–26; Romans 3:24; John 3:16; 1 Peter 5:10; James 4:6; 1 John 4:19)

Scriptures on Grace and Mercy ――――――――――

The LORD is merciful and gracious, slow to anger, and plenteous in mercy.

— PSALM 103:8 KJV

Seeing then that we have a great High Priest who has passed through the heavens, Jesus the Son of God, let us hold fast our confession. For we do not have a High Priest who cannot sympathize with our weaknesses, but was in all points tempted as we are, yet without sin. Let us therefore come boldly to the throne of grace, that we may obtain mercy and find grace to help in time of need.

HEBREWS 4:14–16 NKJV

O give thanks unto the LORD; for he is good: for his mercy endureth for ever.

— PSALM 136:1 KJV

Let the wicked forsake his way, and the unrighteous man his thoughts: and let him return unto the LORD, and he will have mercy upon him; and to our God, for he will abundantly pardon.

— ISAIAH 55:7 KJV

Shouldn't you have mercy on your fellow servant, just as I had mercy on you?

— MATTHEW 18:33 NLT

And his mercy is on them that fear him from generation to generation.

— LUKE 1:50 KJV

For by grace are ye saved through faith; and that not of yourselves: it is the gift of God.

— EPHESIANS 2:8 KJV

Put on therefore, as the elect of God, holy and beloved, bowels of mercies, kindness, humbleness of mind, meekness, longsuffering.

— COLOSSIANS 3:12 KJV

He Would Have a Triumphal Entry

Prophecy:

Rejoice greatly, Daughter Zion! Shout, Daughter Jerusalem! See, your king comes to you, righteous and victorious, lowly and riding on a donkey, on a colt, the foal of a donkey.

— ZECHARIAH 9:9 NIV

Fulfilled:

They took palm branches and went out to meet him, shouting, "Hosanna!" "Blessed is he who comes in the name of the Lord! Blessed is the king of Israel!"

— JOHN 12:13 NIV

6

Forgiveness

My Dear Friend,

My work at the cross cannot be undone. It is the finished work of God's plan. He closed the chapter on the sin of the world that day, and the only thing left for mankind to do is ask for and receive the gift of forgiveness. The Father's forgiveness is final and absolute. When the Father forgives you of a sin, He casts it as far as the east is from the west and forgets it ever happened. The moment you sincerely ask the Father in My name, in light of what I've done for the forgiveness of your sins, then to Him it's as if you had never sinned in the first place.

Forgiveness is a vital part of your relationship with Me, the Holy Spirit, and the Father, as well as with others. I understand it can be difficult to forgive, and that the hurt and pain caused by others can seem overwhelming. But I want you to know I am here for you, and I love you more than you could ever imagine. You do not walk this journey of forgiveness alone. Most importantly, forgiveness is the key to your freedom and true healing.

As My follower, you are called to forgive others, as you have been forgiven. This means letting go of anger and resentment toward those who have hurt you, and choosing to extend grace and compassion to them, just as I have done for you. Forgiveness is not about forgetting what has happened, or about excusing or condoning the actions of others. It is not about allowing yourself to be taken advantage of or permitting others to hurt you again. It's about choosing to let go of the hurt and anger and releasing the person from the debt they owe you. It's about choosing to love and have compassion.

Finally, you must release yourself of the debt of sin. You may still feel bad for your sins and mistakes, even if you remember God has forgotten, but you still need to forgive yourself. It takes faith to trust in your decision and cast the weight of your burden of sin onto My finished work at the cross.

Choosing to forgive is an active decision, a deliberate act that depends not on your feelings at the moment, but on your personal choice. Unforgiveness is like spiritual poison in the wound of your heart; you must get rid of it if your heart is to heal properly. Don't worry or fret when your feelings don't reflect your decision to forgive. Stay the course, and let My love accomplish its perfect work in your heart. Remember, I will be with you every step of the way.

With love,

Jesus

(Hebrews 10:12–14; John 10:28; Romans 5:8; John 19:30; Psalm 103:12; Isaiah 43:25; Hebrews 8:12; 1 John 1:9; Colossians 3:13; Ephesians 4:32; Matthew 6:14–15; Isaiah 43:2)

Scriptures on Forgiveness ————————————————

For if ye forgive men their trespasses, your heavenly Father will also forgive you: But if ye forgive not men their trespasses, neither will your Father forgive your trespasses.

– MATTHEW 6:14–15 KJV

And when ye stand praying, forgive, if ye have ought against any: that your Father also which is in heaven may forgive you your trespasses.

– MARK 11:25 KJV

Judge not, and ye shall not be judged: condemn not, and ye shall not be condemned: forgive, and ye shall be forgiven.

– LUKE 6:37 KJV

Forbearing one another, and forgiving one another, if any man have a quarrel against any: even as Christ forgave you, so also do ye.

– COLOSSIANS 3:13 KJV

And be ye kind one to another, tenderhearted, forgiving one another, even as God for Christ's sake hath forgiven you.

– EPHESIANS 4:32 KJV

For he shall have judgment without mercy, that hath shewed no mercy; and mercy rejoiceth against judgment.

– JAMES 2:13 KJV

But you, Lord, are a compassionate and gracious God, slow to anger, abounding in love and faithfulness.

– PSALM 86:15 NIV

The LORD is merciful and gracious, slow to anger and abounding in steadfast love.

– PSALM 103:8 ESV

He Would Be Betrayed by a Close Friend

Prophecy:

Even my close friend, someone I trusted, one who shared my bread, has turned against me.

— PSALM 41:9 NIV

Fulfilled:

I am not referring to all of you; I know those I have chosen. But this is to fulfill this passage of Scripture: "He who shared my bread has turned against me."

— JOHN 13:18 NIV

7

Prayer

My Beloved,

Prayer is so much more than something you do only when you are in trouble or when you need help or provision. Certainly, it does encompass these things, and these things are essential for your walk upon the earth. But that is not all there is to prayer. Prayer should be a constant and regular part of your life—not for the sake of fulfilling a duty, but for enjoying fellowship with Me.

Prayer is not about saying the right words or performing some kind of ritual; it's about having an open and sincere heart before Me. I see your heart and hear your thoughts, even if you cannot find the words to express them.

Among the most important reasons for Me to come to this earth was to make a way for you to commune with the Father directly. This you may now do through My name and because of My sacrifice. You can now ask the Father anything in My name, in accordance with His will, and the Father will do it for you. This is one of the most joyous realities and experiences that I could ever bring to you and share with you.

Through prayer, you can commune with Me, the Father, and the Holy Spirit. Prayer is the way we can connect with each other. It is how our relationship grows more intimate and personal. No moment you spend in prayer is ever wasted because you are giving your time, attention, and energy to the most important and fulfilling relationship you will ever have. The relationship between you and Me will span from this life into the next. The moment you leave your life on the earth, we will pick up our relationship from there in heaven.

When you and I fellowship as you pray, there are times to be still and listen and times when I would like to speak some things out through you for those around you or in your life. There will also be times of thanksgiving, praise, and worship. As you pray, be sensitive to the voice of the Holy Spirit, and He will take you to deeper places in God.

Remember, I also prayed to My Father while I walked on the earth. I prayed for guidance, for strength, and for wisdom. I've never stopped praying. Even now, on this very day, I pray for you as your Advocate who sits at the right hand of the Father.

Your Brother,

Jesus

(Matthew 21:22; Philippians 4:6–7; Matthew 6:7–8; 1 Thessalonians 5:17; John 14:6; Romans 5:10; Colossians 1:19–20; 1 Peter 3:18; Ephesians 2:13–18; Hebrews 5:7; Romans 8:26–27; Hebrews 10:19–22; 1 Thessalonians 4:17–18; Revelation 21:3–4; Matthew 6:9–13; Matthew 26:36–46; 1 John 2:1; Mark 16:19; Acts 2:33–35; Ephesians 1:20–21; Hebrews 1:3)

Scriptures on Prayer ————————————————

Our Father which art in heaven, hallowed be thy name. Thy kingdom come, thy will be done in earth, as it is in heaven. Give us this day our daily bread. And forgive us our debts, as we forgive our debtors. And lead us not into temptation, but deliver us from evil: for thine is the kingdom, and the power, and the glory, for ever. Amen.

— MATTHEW 6:9–13 KJV

Be careful for nothing; but in every thing by prayer and supplication with thanksgiving let your requests be made known unto God. And the peace of God, which passeth all understanding, shall keep your hearts and minds through Christ Jesus.

— PHILIPPIANS 4:6–7 KJV

Pray without ceasing.

— 1 THESSALONIANS 5:17 KJV

Is any among you afflicted? let him pray. Is any merry? let him sing psalms. Is any sick among you? let him call for the elders of the church; and let them pray over him, anointing him with oil in the name of the Lord: And the prayer of faith shall save the sick, and the Lord shall raise him up; and if he have committed sins, they shall be forgiven him. Confess your faults one to another, and pray one for another, that ye may be healed. The effectual fervent prayer of a righteous man availeth much.

— JAMES 5:13–16 KJV

And this is the confidence that we have in him, that, if we ask any thing according to his will, he heareth us: And if we know that he hear us, whatsoever we ask, we know that we have the petitions that we desired of him.

— 1 JOHN 5:14–15 KJV

He Would Be Despised and Rejected

Prophecy:

He was despised and rejected by mankind, a man of suffering, and familiar with pain. Like one from whom people hide their faces he was despised, and we held him in low esteem.

— Isaiah 53:3 NIV

Fulfilled:

He came to that which was his own, but his own did not receive him.

— John 1:11 NIV

8

God's Word

Dearest Child,

The Bible is not just a book of stories; it is the Word of God, inspired by My Spirit, and it is My voice speaking directly to you. My voice and the words of the Bible are one and the same. As you read its contents, you are familiarizing yourself with My thoughts, My ways, and My voice. So, I urge you to spend time reading, listening to, and meditating upon the Bible.

No other written word has ever been more true, more real, and more powerful than My Word. I infused My very nature and life into its contents. I put within its pages My thoughts, My perspective, My hope for you, and My deepest and sincerest love for you. I will reveal My character to you as you read its pages. I will show you My heart and My will throughout its contents. I will speak to you and reveal to you the way in which you can best live and enjoy life.

My Word is a love letter to all My children. It speaks of the lengths I went through to rescue you. It speaks of the incredible value I have placed on you by paying My own life to buy you back. It speaks of My promises to you, both old and new. It reveals to you what you can expect from Me, what you can ask of Me, and what you can do because of Me.

A supernatural transformation and metamorphosis will happen within you when you determine to make My Word the final authority in your life—when you choose to structure your life on the Word of God and depend on it as your source for stability and confidence. The more you read My Word, the more you meditate on it, and the more you listen to it, the more you will begin to change. Your thoughts will begin to imitate My thoughts. Your actions will begin to imitate My actions. Your faith will begin to grow to imitate My faith. You will begin to know the Father as I know Him. You will begin to see yourself as I see you.

The Bible is not a supplemental book to be read when problems or tests arise in your life. It is not an optional read for your development. It is the very lifeblood of your mission on this earth. It is the essential rock and solid cornerstone on which you are to build your life. It will never falter or fail.

Your King,

Jesus

(2 Timothy 3:16–17; Hebrews 4:12; Psalm 119:105; John 1:1–2; 1 Thessalonians 2:13; Joshua 1:8; Psalm 1:1–3; Ephesians 3:18–19; Psalm 119:9; Romans 12:2; James 1:22–25; 2 Corinthians 3:18; 1 Peter 1:23; Isaiah 55:11; Proverbs 30:5; Isaiah 40:8; Psalm 33:6)

Scriptures on God's Word ————————————————

All Scripture is breathed out by God and profitable for teaching, for reproof, for correction, and for training in righteousness, that the man of God may be complete, equipped for every good work.

– 2 TIMOTHY 3:16–17 ESV

Having been born again, not of corruptible seed but incorruptible, through the word of God which lives and abides forever.

– 1 PETER 1:23 NKJV

Your word is a lamp to my feet and a light to my path.

– PSALM 119:105 ESV

I have hidden your word in my heart that I might not sin against you.

– PSALM 119:11 NIV

So faith comes from hearing, and hearing through the word of Christ.

– ROMANS 10:17 ESV

"Man shall not live by bread alone, but by every word that comes from the mouth of God."

– MATTHEW 4:4 ESV

For the word of God is living and active, sharper than any two-edged sword, piercing to the division of soul and of spirit, of joints and of marrow, and discerning the thoughts and intentions of the heart.

– HEBREWS 4:12 ESV

Therefore, laying aside all malice, all deceit, hypocrisy, envy, and all evil speaking, as newborn babes, desire the pure milk of the word, that you may grow thereby, if indeed you have tasted that the Lord is gracious.

– 1 PETER 2:1–3 NKJV

He Would Be Crucified

Prophecy:

Dogs surround me, a pack of villains encircles me;
they pierce my hands and my feet.

— PSALM 22:16 NIV

Fulfilled:

They crucified him.

— MARK 15:25 NIV

9
The Holy Spirit

My Dear Friend,

When I walked the earth, I promised that the Father would send the Holy Spirit to you. After I left the earth, on the Day of Pentecost, your enemy's worst fears came true. The same Spirit that whipped him—both on the earth and in hell; the same Spirit that he could not overcome, outwit, or stop; the same Spirit of victory and truth; the same Spirit that raised Me from the dead; that same Spirit came upon 120 people in the Upper Room and was made available for all. And so began Satan's worst nightmare, the birth of the Spirit-filled child—you.

Your heavenly Father wanted His relationship with you to be personal. He didn't want you to be separated from Himself for even a second. So, instead of sending an angel to take your concerns before the throne, He sent His very own Spirit. Your body now acts as a temple to house the presence of the Holy Spirit, making it possible for your spirit to commune with the Father intimately and personally. When the Father speaks to you, it is through His Spirit, by which His words and promptings flow.

I do not wish you to be ignorant of the Person of the Holy Spirit, nor would I have you feeling helpless or alone when

His power and companionship are ever available to you. The Holy Spirit is not an optional and additional help in your spiritual walk; He is an essential and integral part of accomplishing the Father's will through you on the earth. My own ministry in the service of the Father did not truly begin until the Holy Spirit came upon Me in the form of a dove. It is the Holy Spirit who brings the life up out of the Word of God and plants it in your heart. It is through the Holy Spirit that revelation flows.

One of the most important things to understand about the Holy Spirit is that He is not a "force"; He is a Person. The Holy Spirit is not some ethereal power you can control or manipulate; He is a living being. It is important to cultivate a personal relationship with the Holy Spirit, allowing Him to guide you and lead you in your daily life.

The Holy Spirit also equips you with spiritual gifts so you can share the love and message of God with others. He also helps to develop you from the inside out until you begin to act like Me, bearing the fruits of love, joy, peace, patience, kindness, goodness, faithfulness, gentleness, and self-control. I encourage you to cultivate a personal relationship with the Holy Spirit, allowing Him to comfort, help, and guide you each and every day.

May our Father bless you,

Jesus

(John 14:16–17; John 16:7–15; Acts 1:8; Acts 2:4; Romans 8:26–27; Galatians 5:22–23; Ephesians 1:13–14; 1 Corinthians 12:4–11; 1 Corinthians 6:19–20; John 15:26; Acts 1:8; Acts 2:1–4)

Scriptures on the Holy Spirit ─────────────

"And I will ask the Father, and he will give you another advocate to help you and be with you forever—the Spirit of truth. The world cannot accept him, because it neither sees him nor knows him. But you know him, for he lives with you and will be in you."

— JOHN 14:16–17 NIV

"Nevertheless I tell you the truth. It is to your advantage that I go away; for if I do not go away, the Helper will not come to you; but if I depart, I will send Him to you. And when He has come, He will convict the world of sin, and of righteousness, and of judgment."

— JOHN 16:7–8 NKJV

Likewise the Spirit helps us in our weakness. For we do not know what to pray for as we ought, but the Spirit himself intercedes for us with groanings too deep for words. And he who searches hearts knows what is the mind of the Spirit, because the Spirit intercedes for the saints according to the will of God.

— ROMANS 8:26–27 ESV

For through him we both have access in one Spirit to the Father.

— EPHESIANS 2:18 ESV

Do you not know that you are the temple of God and that the Spirit of God dwells in you?

— 1 CORINTHIANS 3:16 NKJV

For the Holy One has given you his Spirit, and all of you know the truth.

— 1 JOHN 2:20 NLT

Lots Would Be Cast for His Clothing

Prophecy:

They divide my clothes among them and cast lots for my garment.

— Psalm 22:18 NIV

Fulfilled:

When they had crucified him, they divided up his clothes by casting lots.

— Matthew 27:35 NIV

10

Sin and Redemption

My Dear Believer,

Our Father is the Judge, and as a perfectly just Judge, He demanded, through the conviction of His holy nature, that sin be dealt with in due punishment and payment. We cannot change who we are—the Father, the Holy Spirit, and Myself. We are bound by our nature, our convictions, and our Word. So then, the sin of mankind that Adam committed in the Garden of Eden would have brought about the just and swift end to humanity—if Someone had not stepped in.

You are unique and special to us, and a relationship with you, we determined, was worth the sacrifice it would require to pay in full the price for your sin. So, I laid aside my Godlike glory and power and became as a mortal man. I lived as a man, yet without sin, then I died a sinner's death. I was separated from God, facing eternal damnation, but then I rose again after three days, finally placing My blood on the mercy seat before the Righteous Judge as payment, in full, for the sins of all mankind.

So, believe Me when I say that I have dealt with the sin problem on the earth once and for all. Does this mean you will never sin again? No. Does this mean the punishment you should receive for that sin has already been dealt with? Yes.

To receive the gift of My redemption and forgiveness, you must first take responsibility for your actions. All have sinned against the Father, and all have fallen short of His glory. The act of going before the Father in My name to seek forgiveness for your sins is an act of obedience and submission to Me and the Father. You must submit yourself to Our authority, Our law, and Our ways, and you must obey Us by asking for the Father's forgiveness as I've instructed in My Word. That simple act activates the power of My blood at the mercy seat, and the Father will immediately cast your sins from you in that very moment.

So, there is no need to feel as if you are under condemnation for another second. If you will come to Me, and follow Me, even as I followed the Father on the earth, then you need not feel unloved or condemned another day in your life. Condemnation will come, but it is not from Me. It is a tactic from the enemy, who seeks to create a barrier between you and Me. He knows that if he can separate you from Me, you will become an easy mark. Don't let him succeed. Stay close to Me, take refuge in Me, and believe in what I have said, even more than what you may be feeling. Then you will see your peace restored and joy overflow in your life.

With love,

Jesus

(Psalm 75:7; Hebrews 12:23; Romans 3:23–24; Romans 1:20; Matthew 5:18; Romans 5; Philippians 2:5–8; Hebrews 4:15; 2 Corinthians 5:21; Galatians 3:13; 1 Peter 2:24; Isaiah 53:5–6; 1 John 1:9; Proverbs 28:13; Acts 4:12; Romans 10:9–10; Micah 7:18–19; Isaiah 1:18; Psalm 103:12; Romans 8:1; Psalm 46:1)

Scriptures on Sin and Redemption ——————————

If we [freely] admit that we have sinned and confess our sins, He is faithful and just (true to His own nature and promises) and will forgive our sins [dismiss our lawlessness] and [continuously] cleanse us from all unrighteousness [everything not in conformity to His will in purpose, thought, and action].

— 1 JOHN 1:9 AMPC

But God demonstrates his own love for us in this: While we were still sinners, Christ died for us.

— ROMANS 5:8 NIV

Therefore, if anyone is in Christ, the new creation has come: The old has gone, the new is here!

— 2 CORINTHIANS 5:17 NIV

"And I will give you a new heart, and a new spirit I will put within you. And I will remove the heart of stone from your flesh and give you a heart of flesh."

— EZEKIEL 36:26 ESV

For our sake He made Christ [virtually] to be sin Who knew no sin, so that in and through Him we might become [endued with, viewed as being in, and examples of] the righteousness of God [what we ought to be, approved and acceptable and in right relationship with Him, by His goodness].

— 2 CORINTHIANS 5:21 AMPC

Yet it was our weaknesses he carried; it was our sorrows that weighed him down. And we thought his troubles were a punishment from God, a punishment for his own sins! But he was pierced for our rebellion, crushed for our sins. He was beaten so we could be whole. He was whipped so we could be healed. All of us, like sheep, have strayed away. We have left God's paths to follow our own. Yet the LORD laid on him the sins of us all.

— ISAIAH 53:4–6 NLT

Not a Bone of His Would Be Broken

Prophecy:

He protects all his bones, not one of them will be broken.

— PSALM 34:20 NIV

Fulfilled:

But when they came to Jesus and found that he was already dead, they did not break his legs.

— JOHN 19:33 NIV

11

Wisdom

My Dear Friend,

I come to you today to speak of something incredibly precious. She is the principal thing. Her value is greater than that of gold, silver, or precious gems. She has length of days in her right hand and riches and honor in her left. Her name is Wisdom. Child, many seek knowledge and understanding, but true wisdom is a rare and precious thing. It is not something that can be attained through mere study or intellect, but rather it comes through humility, patience, and a simple request of it from the Father.

Wisdom is not something that can be grasped by the mind alone; rather, it is a gift from God, given to those who are willing to seek it and ask for it. True wisdom is not found in the words of men, but in the Word of God. It is not found in the wisdom of this world, but in the wisdom of the Spirit.

To attain wisdom, you must humble yourself before God, then ask Him for wisdom. This request does not mean getting a "second opinion" to that of your own or trying to get God's "stamp of approval" on what you are already wanting to do. It is the process of seeking how God would handle any situation. It means coming to Him with an open mind, eager to sit and listen at the Father's feet.

So, exercise your faith and patience. Wisdom may not always come overnight, but you have My word that if you ask for it and do not doubt in your heart, you will receive it. If it seems as though wisdom, or hearing My voice, doesn't come easy to you, then "tune up" on My Word. My Word is Wisdom and Truth. I am indistinguishable from it, and our voices are one and the same. The more you listen to and read My Word, the more accustomed you will become at hearing and recognizing it.

Many ask to hear a "word" from Me when they haven't spent the time to read what I've already said to them in My Word. If your situation is dire, come to Me and I will help. When I provide the peace you so desperately need, then use it to study Me and My Word, allowing it to shape your understanding of this world. Learn and recognize My ways and My words.

My friend, wisdom is not something to be taken lightly. It is a precious gift from God. May you seek wisdom with all your heart, and may you find it in the Word of God. May you grow in knowledge and understanding, and may you be guided by the wisdom of the Spirit. May you always remember that true wisdom is not found in the words of men, but in the Word of God.

With love and blessings,

Jesus

(Proverbs 4:7; Proverbs 1:7; Proverbs 16:16; Proverbs 3:13–16; Proverbs 2:6; Ecclesiastes 7:12; Colossians 3:16; Proverbs 8:11; Psalm 111:10; Proverbs 11:2; James 4:6; James 1:5–6; Mark 11:24)

Scriptures on Wisdom ────────────────

Blessed are those who find wisdom, those who gain understanding, for she is more profitable than silver and yields better returns than gold.

— Proverbs 3:13–14 NIV

Wisdom is supreme; therefore get wisdom. Though it cost all you have, get understanding.

— Proverbs 4:7 NIV 1984

If any of you lacks wisdom, let him ask God, who gives generously to all without reproach, and it will be given him. But let him ask in faith, with no doubting, for the one who doubts is like a wave of the sea that is driven and tossed by the wind.

— James 1:5–6 ESV

The Spirit of the Lord will rest on him—the Spirit of wisdom and of understanding, the Spirit of counsel and of might, the Spirit of the knowledge and fear of the Lord.

— Isaiah 11:2 NIV

In [Christ] are hidden all the treasures of wisdom and knowledge.

— Colossians 2:3 NIV

The fear of the Lord is the beginning of wisdom: and the knowledge of the holy is understanding.

— Proverbs 9:10 KJV

How much better to get wisdom than gold, to choose understanding rather than silver!

— Proverbs 16:16 NIV 1984

The fear of the Lord is the beginning of wisdom; all who follow his precepts have good understanding. To him belongs eternal praise.

— Psalm 111:10 NIV

His Side Would Be Pierced

Prophecy:

They will look on me, the one they have pierced.

— ZECHARIAH 12:10 NIV

Fulfilled:

Instead, one of the soldiers pierced Jesus' side with a spear, bringing a sudden flow of blood and water.

— JOHN 19:34 NIV

12

A Proclamation from the King to His Citizens

My Beloved Citizen of Heaven,

I, King Jesus, address you today with a message of hope and assurance. I know that you have been waiting for My return, and I assure you the time is near. But I also implore you to be patient, for there is still much work to be done before I can gather you to Me.

As your King, it is My duty to guide and protect you, to lead you on the path of righteousness, and to bring you to the eternal glory that awaits you in My Kingdom. I assure you, My dear citizen, I am doing everything in My power to make that day come as soon as possible.

But to bring about this day, the task is not all on Me. I also ask for your help. I ask that you remain steadfast in your faith, that you continue to live your life in accordance with My Word, and that you continue to spread the word of My Gospel to all. Together, we can bring about My soon return.

I know you may have questions about the end times, about the nature of My return, and about what will happen to those who are left behind. But I assure you, My dear citizen, that all will be made clear in due time. You know Me. You know how I work. So, trust Me.

In the meantime, I'd like to remind you where your loyalties and protections lie. You may occupy a nation currently on the earth, but your true citizenship is in heaven! I am your King, and you have access to My riches in glory. You have access to My army of angels, activated for your protection. You have access to Me, and I've granted you an audience with the King at any time you desire. Do not be afraid to draw on your heavenly resources as My ambassador to the world.

And so, I urge you, My beloved citizen of heaven, to be patient and to have faith. The day of My return is coming soon, and together we will usher in a new era of peace, love, and glory. I will gather you to Me, and we will reign together for all eternity. So be strong, be courageous, and know I am with you always. Together, we will overcome all obstacles, and enjoy a beautiful relationship together in heaven.

By righteous decree, your King,

Jesus

(1 Timothy 6:15; Revelation 17:14; Revelation 19:16; James 5:7–8; Matthew 24:14; 2 Peter 3:9–10; Mark 13:10; Revelation 7:9–10; Romans 10:14–15; Romans 5:3–5; Romans 8:25; Hebrews 6:11–12; Isaiah 26:4; Philippians 3:20; Hebrews 1:14; Ephesians 1:3; Matthew 6:33; Philippians 4:19; Ephesians 3:16; Colossians 1:27; Revelation 22:12; 1 Thessalonians 4:16–17; Titus 2:13; Revelation 21:4; 2 Peter 3:13; John 16:33)

Scriptures on a Proclamation from the King to His Citizens

For the Lord himself will come down from heaven with a commanding shout, with the voice of the archangel, and with the trumpet call of God. First, the believers who have died will rise from their graves. Then, together with them, we who are still alive and remain on the earth will be caught up in the clouds to meet the Lord in the air. Then we will be with the Lord forever.

— 1 THESSALONIANS 4:16–17 NLT

"Therefore you also must be ready, for the Son of Man is coming at an hour you do not expect."

— MATTHEW 24:44 ESV

The Lord is not slow to fulfill his promise as some count slowness, but is patient toward you, not wishing that any should perish, but that all should reach repentance.

— 2 PETER 3:9 ESV

He which testifieth these things saith, Surely I come quickly. Amen. Even so, come, Lord Jesus.

— REVELATION 22:20 KJV

For I consider that the sufferings of this present time are not worth comparing with the glory that is to be revealed to us. For the creation waits with eager longing for the revealing of the sons of God. For the creation was subjected to futility, not willingly, but because of him who subjected it, in hope that the creation itself will be set free from its bondage to corruption and obtain the freedom of the glory of the children of God.

— ROMANS 8:18–21 ESV

"Watch therefore, for you know neither the day nor the hour in which the Son of Man is coming."

— MATTHEW 25:13 NKJV

He Would Be Buried in a Rich Man's Tomb

Prophecy:

He was assigned a grave with the wicked, and with the rich in his death.

— Isaiah 53:9 NIV

Fulfilled:

Going to Pilate, he asked for Jesus' body, and Pilate ordered that it be given to him. Joseph took the body, wrapped it in a clean linen cloth, and placed it in his own new tomb that he had cut out of the rock.

— Matthew 27:58–60 NIV

13

A Letter to Remind You Who You Are

My Dear Friend,

I am writing to you today to remind you of who you truly are. You are a new creation, made new by the power of My love and grace. Old things have passed away, and all things have become new. You are strong. You may feel weak and powerless at times, but faith is not a feeling, and I have given you the strength you need to overcome any obstacle that comes your way.

You are also a light in the darkness. I have called you to be a beacon of hope and love to those around you. You are to shine My light and love into the world, bringing hope to the hopeless and love to the unloved. You are a child of God. Our Father has adopted you as His very own, and you are now a part of My family. You have been given all the rights and privileges as one of His children. You are His beloved, and I will always love and care for you as your Brother.

You have been chosen by Me. I have chosen you for a purpose, to bring My love and light to the world. You are righteous because of Me. I have made you right with God through My sacrifice on the cross. You are an ambassador of Mine, representing Me to the world. You are to share the Good News of My love and grace with those around you, drawing upon My resources to get the job done. You are redeemed, bought back by My blood. You were once a slave to sin, but I have set you free and made you My very own. I have paid the price for your redemption, and you are now Mine. You are complete in Me. I am the Source of your completeness, and I will always be enough for you. You do not need to look for anything else to make you complete, for I am all you need. You are protected by Me. I am your shelter and your refuge. I will keep you safe from all harm, and I will never leave you, nor forsake you.

You are more than a conqueror through Me. I have given you the power to overcome any obstacle that comes your way. I have already won the victory, and you are victorious in Me. Finally, you are the temple of the Holy Spirit. I have sent My Spirit to dwell within you, to guide you and empower you. You are a holy and sacred vessel, set apart for My use. My dear friend, remember who you are in Me. Live in that reality, and walk in the freedom and power I have given you. Go forth and make a difference in the world, shining My light and love for all to see.

Affectionately yours,

Jesus

(2 Corinthians 5:17; Philippians 4:13; Matthew 5:14; John 1:12; John 15:16; 2 Corinthians 5:21; 2 Corinthians 5:20; Ephesians 1:7; Colossians 2:10; Psalm 121:7–8; Romans 8:17; Romans 8:37; 1 Corinthians 6:19; Hebrews 13:5; Isaiah 40:29; Ephesians 1:5; Romans 5:1; Mark 16:15; Romans 6:22; 2 Corinthians 12:9; 1 John 4:4; John 14:16–17; Ephesians 6:10; 2 Timothy 2:21; Philippians 4:19; 1 Corinthians 15:57; 1 Peter 1:18–19; John 14:8; Deuteronomy 31:8; Matthew 28:19)

Scriptures on Who You Are —————————————

Therefore, if anyone is in Christ, he is a new creation; the old has gone, the new has come!

— 2 CORINTHIANS 5:17 NIV 1984

It is for freedom that Christ has set us free. Stand firm, then, and do not let yourselves be burdened again by a yoke of slavery.

— GALATIANS 5:1 NIV

I can do all things through Christ who strengthens me.

— PHILIPPIANS 4:13 NKJV

"You are the light of the world. A city on a hill cannot be hidden."

— MATTHEW 5:14 NIV 1984

But to all who did receive him, who believed in his name, he gave the right to become children of God.

— JOHN 1:12 ESV

For he chose us in him before the creation of the world to be holy and blameless in his sight.

— EPHESIANS 1:4 NIV

Therefore, we are ambassadors for Christ, God making his appeal through us.... For our sake he made him to be sin who knew no sin, so that in him we might become the righteousness of God.

— 2 CORINTHIANS 5:20–21 ESV

In him we have redemption through his blood, the forgiveness of our trespasses, according to the riches of his grace.

— EPHESIANS 1:7 ESV

Do you not know that your bodies are temples of the Holy Spirit, who is in you, whom you have received from God? You are not your own.

— 1 CORINTHIANS 6:19 NIV

He Would Be Resurrected

Prophecy:

For you will not abandon my soul to Sheol, or let your holy one see corruption.

— PSALM 16:10 ESV

Fulfilled:

"He is not here; he has risen, just as he said. Come and see the place where he lay."

— MATTHEW 28:6 NIV

14

Be Thankful

Dearest Child,

As I sit here in the heavens, I am filled with overwhelming gratitude for your life. Each day, I am reminded of the love and grace I have for you, and it brings Me great joy to see you living your life in such a way that brings glory to the Father in heaven.

I want to take this opportunity to remind you of the importance of thankfulness in your life. It can be easy to forget the many blessings you have been given when you focus on the wrong things. I urge you to take time each day to reflect on the things for which you are thankful. Whether it is the love of a family member, the beauty of nature, or the simple pleasures of life, there is always something for which you can be grateful. If nothing else, if you didn't receive any help or blessings available to you except the gift of salvation, that should be enough for you to rejoice the rest of your days, living in complete bliss. Escaping hell and spending eternity in heaven with Me is worth celebrating! In fact, there is a party up here every time another person decides to join My family!

Thankfulness is not just a feeling or an emotion; it is also an attitude you should strive to nurture in your heart. Even in the midst of difficult circumstances, you can choose to focus on the good and remain thankful for the blessings I have given you. This is not always easy, but with the help of the Holy Spirit, you can learn to see the world through a lens of gratitude. In doing this, you will be cultivating a lifestyle of thanksgiving. Instead of walking through life aware of the daily challenges, fatigue, and problems that come with living on the earth, you will walk through life in light of My blessings, support, and companionship. In short, you'll be walking by faith and not by sight. What greater expression of faith is there than to lift up your voice to Me in triumphant and joyous gratitude in the midst of the worst life has to offer?

Let Me be clear: Never thank Me for the problems; always thank Me for the solutions! Never thank Me for pain, sickness, or cruelty. I am not the author of such things. I have come that you may have life and have it in abundance! In addition to the blessings you have been given, you should also be thankful for the opportunities that you have to serve and love others. Each day, you have the opportunity to make a difference in the lives of those around you, whether it is through simple acts of kindness or more significant actions. Do not take these opportunities for granted, but instead see them as a way to glorify the Father and bring hope and joy to those in need.

In closing, child of God, I urge you to take time each day to reflect on the things for which you are truly thankful. Focus on the good, not the bad. Cultivate a lifestyle of gratitude.

With love and blessings,

Jesus

(Colossians 3:15; Ephesians 2:8–9; John 14:2–3; 1 Thessalonians 5:18; Ephesians 5:20; Matthew 11:28; James 1:17; Galatians 5:13; Philippians 4:8; Philippians 4:6; Lamentations 3:33; 1 Corinthians 14:33; John 10:10)

Scriptures on Thankfulness ———————————————

Enter into his gates with thanksgiving, and into his courts with praise: be thankful unto him, and bless his name.

— PSALM 100:4 KJV

Let the peace of Christ rule in your hearts, since as members of one body you were called to peace. And be thankful.

— COLOSSIANS 3:15 NIV

Thank [God] in everything [no matter what the circumstances may be, be thankful and give thanks], for this is the will of God for you [who are] in Christ Jesus [the Revealer and Mediator of that will].

— 1 THESSALONIANS 5:18 AMPC

Giving thanks always and for everything to God the Father in the name of our Lord Jesus Christ.

— EPHESIANS 5:20 ESV

Do not be anxious about anything, but in every situation, by prayer and petition, with thanksgiving, present your requests to God.

— PHILIPPIANS 4:6 NIV

Give thanks to the LORD, for he is good; his love endures forever.

— PSALM 107:1 NIV

The one who offers thanksgiving as his sacrifice glorifies me; to one who orders his way rightly I will show the salvation of God!

— PSALM 50:23 ESV

He Would Ascend to the Right Hand of God

Prophecy:

The LORD says to my lord: "Sit at my right hand until I make your enemies a footstool for your feet."

— PSALM 110:1 NIV

Fulfilled:

After the Lord Jesus had spoken to them, he was taken up into heaven and he sat at the right hand of God.

— MARK 16:19 NIV

15

Remember Who I Am

My Dear Friend,

I am Jesus, the Son of God and the King of kings. I come to you today to remind you of who I am and what that means for you.

In Me, God's Word took on human nature to reconcile you to Himself, to show you His nature, to demonstrate His love, and to provide the ultimate sacrifice for your sins. I am both fully God and fully human. As God, I am eternal, omnipotent, and holy. As human, I was born, grew, felt hunger, experienced joy and sorrow, and died. Through this, I have bridged the vast gap between us. I am the living and breathing testament of God's love and grace, who understands your struggles, your joys, your fears, and your hopes.

I am the way, the truth, and the life. No one comes to the Father except through Me. I am the only path to salvation and eternal life. I am the One who died on the cross for your sins and rose again to give you new life. I am the One who now sits at the right hand of the Father, interceding for you and pleading your case before Him.

I am your High Priest. I understand and sympathize with the struggles and challenges that you face in this life. I have been through it all, and I know what it is like to be human and to suffer. But I also know the love and grace of the Father, and I offer that to you. Come to Me with your burdens, and I will give you rest.

I am the Author and Finisher of your faith. I am the One who began the good work in you, and I am the One who will bring it to completion. Trust in Me and My power to work in your life. I will guide you and strengthen you as you walk with Me.

I am also the Prince of Peace. In a world full of chaos and turmoil, I offer you the peace that surpasses all understanding. I am the shelter from the storm, and I am always with you, even in the darkest of times.

I urge you to remember who I am and what that means for you. I am all that I have said; simply realize what that means to you. I am not just a historical figure or a religious leader; I am your leader, and you are part of My family. I am not just the Son of God and the Savior of the world; I am your Brother, and I am your Savior. I am not just a king and lord above all others; I am your King and your Lord. No name, authority, or decree shall rise above My own, and I reside over you. Who is it who will take you from My jurisdiction? There is none.

Sincerely,

Jesus

(Revelation 19:16; John 3:16; Psalm 47:7; John 14:6; Romans 4:25; Romans 8:34; John 1:14; Philippians 4:7; Hebrews 4:15; Hebrews 12:2; Ephesians 3:20; Philippians 1:6; Isaiah 9:6; Revelation 17:14; Matthew 11:28; Ephesians 2:19; Hebrews 2:11; Philippians 2:9–11; Colossians 1:27; Galatians 2:20; John 10:10; Romans 8:38–39)

Scriptures on Who Jesus Is ———————————

"I am the way, the truth, and the life. No one comes to the Father except through Me."

— JOHN 14:6 NKJV

For we do not have a high priest who is unable to sympathize with our weaknesses, but one who in every respect has been tempted as we are, yet without sin.

— HEBREWS 4:15 ESV

For to us a child is born, to us a son is given; and the government shall be upon his shoulder, and his name shall be called Wonderful Counselor, Mighty God, Everlasting Father, Prince of Peace.

— ISAIAH 9:6 ESV

In the beginning [before all time] was the Word (Christ), and the Word was with God, and the Word was God Himself. He was present originally with God. All things were made and came into existence through Him; and without Him was not even one thing made that has come into being. In Him was Life, and the Life was the Light of men.

— JOHN 1:1–4 AMPC

For there is one God and one Mediator between God and men, the Man Christ Jesus.

— 1 TIMOTHY 2:5 NKJV

"Teaching them to observe all things whatsoever I have commanded you: and, lo, I am with you always, even unto the end of the world. Amen."

— MATTHEW 28:20 KJV

He Would Be the Cornertone

Prophecy:

The stone the builders rejected has become the cornerstone.

— Psalm 118:22 NIV

Fulfilled:

Jesus said to them, "Have you never read in the Scriptures: 'The stone the builders rejected has become the cornerstone; the Lord has done this, and it is marvelous in our eyes'?"

— Matthew 21:42 NIV

16

Finances

My Dear Friend,

I understand the subject of finances can be a source of stress and worry for many people. I will take care of you. You are valuable to Me. Many times, the distress you feel is not the problem itself, but your estimation of it. Esteem Me greater. Look at the birds. Do they work for a living? Do they have bank accounts? Do they labor and toil and worry over food and clothes and provision? Don't I see to it that they are fed? Dear child, their value is not even comparable to that of your own. Quit stressing out and worrying. Take it one day at a time. Trust Me.

When you get too focused on money, you open yourself up to all sorts of problems. Loving money is the root of all sorts of evil on the earth. Many think that if you are poor, then that means you must be holy. That's not true. You could not have any money and love it more than someone who is very wealthy. The point is, how much of your day are you concerned about your finances? How much of your life is being consumed by your lack of money or your accumulation of it?

My friend, that is no way to live your life! Tithe off all your income. Be generous, as I have been generous with you. I became poor on this earth so that you could be rich. Poverty and lack do not honor Me; I want better for you than that. Be a good steward of the resources I have given you. This means being wise and responsible in your spending and saving, being generous with your money and resources, and being content with what you have. Remember, the Father will always provide for your needs.

The Kingdom doesn't work like the world. In the world, if you want more, then you must take more and save more. In My Kingdom, it works the other way around. If you want to be trusted with more finances, then you must give more away. If you want to be trusted in greater levels of leadership in My Kingdom, then you must serve more. Remember to be a good steward of what I've given you, and remain willing to give anything that I should ask you for, for the sake of the Kingdom.

Don't be afraid to come to Me when things are tight, and I'll alleviate the problem. If I'll take care of the birds in the sky, then you should rest assured that I'll take care of you.

May the blessings of our Father be upon you and your finances,

Jesus

(Matthew 6:25–34; 1 Timothy 6:10; Matthew 6:24; Ecclesiastes 5:10; Proverbs 23:4–5; Luke 12:15; Proverbs 10:22; Deuteronomy 8:18; Titus 1:7; Titus 1:11; Malachi 3:10; Matthew 10:8; Luke 6:38; 2 Corinthians 9:6; Proverbs 11:25; Acts 20:35; Proverbs 3:9–10; Proverbs 19:17; 2 Corinthians 8:9; Proverbs 22:9; Galatians 6:9–10; 1 Corinthians 4:2; Luke 16:10–11; 1 Peter 4:10–11; Matthew 25:14–30; 1 Timothy 6:17–18; Matthew 20:26–28; Mark 9:35; Luke 22:26)

Scriptures on Finances ─────────────────────

And God is able to make all grace [every favor and earthly bless-
ing] come in abundance to you, so that you may always [under all
circumstances, regardless of the need] have complete sufficiency
in everything [being completely self-sufficient in Him], and have
an abundance for every good work and act of charity.

— 2 CORINTHIANS 9:8 AMP

And [God] Who provides seed for the sower and bread for eating
will also provide and multiply your [resources for] sowing and
increase the fruits of your righteousness [which manifests itself in
active goodness, kindness, and charity]. Thus you will be enriched
in all things and in every way, so that you can be generous, and
[your generosity as it is] administered by us will bring forth
thanksgiving to God.

— 2 CORINTHIANS 9:10–11 AMPC

And my God will meet all your needs according to the riches of
his glory in Christ Jesus.

— PHILIPPIANS 4:19 NIV

He gives food to those who fear him; he always remembers his
covenant.

— PSALM 111:5 NLT

"Give, and it will be given to you. They will pour into your lap a
good measure—pressed down, shaken together, and running over
[with no space left for more]. For with the standard of measure-
ment you use [when you do good to others], it will be measured
to you in return."

— LUKE 6:38 AMP

Keep your lives free from the love of money and be content with
what you have, because God has said, "Never will I leave you;
never will I forsake you."

— HEBREWS 13:5 NIV

He Would Come in the Name of the Lord

Prophecy:

Blessed is he who comes in the name of the Lord.

— Psalm 118:26 NIV

Fulfilled:

The crowds that went ahead of him and those that followed shouted, "Hosanna to the Son of David! Blessed is he who comes in the name of the Lord! Hosanna in the highest heaven!"

— Matthew 21:9 NIV

17

Protection

Dear Beloved,

I write to you today to assure you of My protection. I am your Rock, a firm foundation upon which you can build your life. I will not falter. I will not rattle or shake. I am everlasting and immovable. When you depend on Me, when you stand on My Word, then even though the storms of life may crash against you, you will not be destroyed. When you partake of Me, of the Father, and of the Holy Spirit, you partake of Our stability. There is a steadiness that accompanies Our presence, a surety that accompanies Our companionship. Lean on Me as your Rock, and you will outlast any storm.

I am your shield. You do have an enemy, and you are within enemy territory. You are My ambassador to a world that is in rebellion. There are a thousand ways the enemy wants to destroy you, steal from you, or kill you. I am what prevents him from doing so. Perhaps one of the greatest testimonies you can give is that you are still here. You are still breathing. Don't you think that if given the opportunity, the enemy of your soul would have taken you out? Of course he would have, but I wouldn't let him.

I am your Refuge and Fortress. When you need to rest in a safe place, come and rest in Me. When you need a reprieve from the dangers of this world, come and recover in My presence. When the ever-present stresses and pressures begin to beat against you, retreat against My wall and cast those cares on Me.

My friend, even now, as you read these words, I am with you, watching over you and keeping you safe. I am your Protector, your Guide, and your Friend. I am with you in every moment, through every day. Take My hand and follow Me. You may not always see or feel My presence, but I assure you I am always with you. I am always watching over you and keeping you safe. I know the troubles and struggles you are facing, and I am with you every step of the way.

I urge you to trust in Me, to let Me be your Protector by asking Me for My help and attaching your faith to this truth. I will guide you through the darkest of times, and I will light your way through the storms of life. I will be your strength when you are weak and your refuge when you are afraid.

I promise that if you let Me, I will continue to protect you all the days of your life.

Yours always,

Jesus

(Psalm 18:2; Psalm 91:1–2; Matthew 7:24–25; Isaiah 40:8; Psalm 18:30; Proverbs 18:10; Isaiah 41:10; 2 Thessalonians 3:3; Psalm 34:7; 2 Corinthians 4:8–9; Matthew 11:28–30; 2 Timothy 4:18; 1 John 4:4; Psalm 46:1; Psalm 62:7–8; Proverbs 14:26; Nahum 1:7; Psalm 121:5–8; Isaiah 43:2)

Scriptures on Protection

He is my loving God and my fortress, my stronghold and my deliverer, my shield, in whom I take refuge, who subdues peoples under me.

– PSALM 144:2 NIV

He who dwells in the secret place of the Most High shall abide under the shadow of the Almighty. I will say of the LORD, "He is my refuge and my fortress; my God, in Him I will trust."

– PSALM 91:1–2 NKJV

For he will command his angels concerning you to guard you in all your ways.

– PSALM 91:11 ESV

"For I am the LORD your God who takes hold of your right hand and says to you, Do not fear; I will help you."

– ISAIAH 41:13 NIV

"Be strong and courageous. Do not be afraid or terrified because of them, for the LORD your God goes with you; he will never leave you nor forsake you."

– DEUTERONOMY 31:6 NIV

"No weapon forged against you will prevail, and you will refute every tongue that accuses you. This is the heritage of the servants of the LORD, and this is their vindication from me," declares the LORD.

– ISAIAH 54:17 NIV

"I have given you authority to trample on snakes and scorpions and to overcome all the power of the enemy; nothing will harm you."

– LUKE 10:19 NIV

He Would Be a Prophet Like Moses

Prophecy:

"The Lord your God will raise up for you a prophet like me from among you, from your fellow Israelites. You must listen to him."

— Deuteronomy 18:15 NIV

Fulfilled:

"But do not think I will accuse you before the Father. Your accuser is Moses, on whom your hopes are set. If you believed Moses, you would believe me, for he wrote about me. But since you do not believe what he wrote, how are you going to believe what I say?"

— John 5:45–47 NIV

18

God's Power

Dear Child,

I come to you today to speak of the power that lies within you. For too long, you have felt weak, insignificant, and powerless in the face of the world's trials and tribulations. But I tell you, my dear one, you are not weak, you are not insignificant, and you are not powerless.

The power that lies within you is the power of love. It is the power that can conquer all fear, all hatred, and all division. It is the power that can heal the sick, comfort the mourning, and bring hope to the hopeless. This power is not something that can be grasped or held on to. It is not something that can be bought or sold. It is not something that can be earned or taken away. It is a gift, given freely to you by My Father in heaven.

And yet, some people choose to reject this gift, opting instead to rely on the fleeting and temporary powers of this world. Some seek power in wealth, in status, in fame, and in control over others. But these powers will always fall short, leaving those who have grasped them empty and unfulfilled. The true power—the power of love—comes from within. It is a power rooted in humility, service, and sacrifice. It is a power that is demonstrated in the way you treat others, in the way you speak, and in the way you live your life.

I urge you, my dear friend, to let go of the false powers of this world and embrace the true power of love. Allow it to guide your thoughts, your words, and your actions. Allow it to transform your heart and change the way you see the world. In doing so, you will find you are capable of bringing light to the darkness, hope to the hopeless, and love to the unloved.

Do not be afraid to use this power, my dear one. Do not be afraid to speak out against injustice, to stand up for the oppressed, and to love the unlovable. For in doing so, you will be fulfilling the purpose for which you were created and bringing glory to My Father in heaven.

I am with you always, dear child. I am with you in your joy and in your sorrow. I am with you in your successes and in your failures. I am with you in your struggles and in your triumphs.

Remember, the true power is within you. Allow it to guide you, transform you, and change the world.

With My love,

Jesus

(Philippians 4:13; 2 Corinthians 12:9; Ephesians 3:20; Romans 8:37; Matthew 10:29–31; Romans 8:31; Mark 8:36; Matthew 6:19–21; 1 Timothy 6:9–10; Micah 6:8; Matthew 5:16; Matthew 25:40; Ephesians 2:10; Psalm 23:4)

Scriptures on God's Power ————————————

And if the Spirit of Him Who raised up Jesus from the dead dwells in you, [then] He Who raised up Christ Jesus from the dead will also restore to life your mortal (short-lived, perishable) bodies through His Spirit Who dwells in you.

— ROMANS 8:11 AMPC

But the fruit of the Spirit is love, joy, peace, patience, kindness, goodness, faithfulness, gentleness, self-control; against such things there is no law.

— GALATIANS 5:22–23 ESV

That's why I work and struggle so hard, depending on Christ's mighty power that works within me.

— COLOSSIANS 1:29 NLT

Love is patient and kind; love does not envy or boast; it is not arrogant or rude. It does not insist on its own way; it is not irritable or resentful; it does not rejoice at wrongdoing, but rejoices with the truth. Love bears all things, believes all things, hopes all things, endures all things.

— 1 CORINTHIANS 13:4–7 ESV

I have strength for all things in Christ Who empowers me [I am ready for anything and equal to anything through Him Who infuses inner strength into me; I am self-sufficient in Christ's sufficiency].

— PHILIPPIANS 4:13 AMPC

And now these three remain: faith, hope and love. But the greatest of these is love.

— 1 CORINTHIANS 13:13 NIV

"A new commandment I give to you, that you love one another: just as I have loved you, you also are to love one another."

— JOHN 13:34 ESV

He Would Usher In a New Covenant

Prophecy:

"The days are coming," declares the Lord, "when I will make a new covenant with the people of Israel and with the people of Judah."

— JEREMIAH 31:31 NIV

Fulfilled:

In the same way, after the supper he took the cup, saying, "This cup is the new covenant in my blood, which is poured out for you."

— LUKE 22:20 NIV

19

Joy

My Dear Sibling,

My joy is so much more than just being happy or contented with your circumstances. Joy is not a thought or an emotion. Real, genuine joy, much like My peace, is a state of being. It is a sweet disposition that fuels your faith and strengthens your very core. Through time spent with Me in prayer and in the reading, listening, and contemplation of My Word, you begin to align your perspective to the truth of your situation. You are far better off than you have realized up till now.

As a child of the Most High God, you needn't spend another day without My joy! Your situation has never been better in all of time and eternity. You are an adopted member of My family, and I have told you repeatedly that I will help you and take care of you. Spend time with Me until that revelation drops deep into your heart. Then hold on to your confidence in Me for dear life! Never let it go, despite what you may see in this world, and you will live in the strength of My joy. There is no test, trial, problem, or issue in life that can ever force you into submission or rob you of your peace and joy. The only way you will lose your peace, your joy, or your confidence is when you cast them away through esteeming other things besides Me.

I understand it can be easy to become overwhelmed by the troubles of this world. All you have to do is spend some time focusing on your circumstances instead of Me. Staying in My joy is a choice—and a daily one at that. It is a decision not to falter or become fearful at the first sign of opposition. It's the choice to smile in your heart despite the problems of the day because of your trust in My goodness. Get to know Me and My character and see My overwhelming desire throughout My Word to see you healthy, prosperous, at peace, and full of joy!

My joy inside you will strengthen you and sustain you. It will cause you to walk on the bright side of life. It will cause you to look up at the sky and enjoy the sunshine. It will help you see life in a brighter and more vibrant way than you have ever seen it before. I wish this for you. I wish for you to see the beauty in your situation instead of the muck and mire produced by a world in sin and rebellion. So, meditate on My goodness and allow My joy to bubble up from within you and change your life.

Your Friend,

Jesus

(Psalm 16:11; Psalm 30:5; Psalm 51:12; Isaiah 9:3; Isaiah 12:3; Isaiah 55:12; Romans 15:13; Galatians 5:22–23; Philippians 4:4; 1 Peter 1:8–9; Nehemiah 8:10; John 15:11; Galatians 4:4–7; Hebrews 10:35; James 1:2–4; Colossians 1:11)

Scriptures on Joy

"These things I have spoken to you, that my joy may be in you, and that your joy may be full."

— JOHN 15:11 ESV

I pray that God, the source of hope, will fill you completely with joy and peace because you trust in him. Then you will overflow with confident hope through the power of the Holy Spirit.

— ROMANS 15:13 NLT

The joy of the LORD is your strength!

— NEHEMIAH 8:10 ESV

Consider it pure joy, my brothers and sisters, whenever you face trials of many kinds, because you know that the testing of your faith produces perseverance.

— JAMES 1:2–3 NIV

Rejoice in the Lord always. I will say it again: Rejoice!

— PHILIPPIANS 4:4 NIV

You will show me the path of life; in Your presence is fullness of joy; at Your right hand are pleasures forevermore.

— PSALM 16:11 NKJV

And not only that, but we also glory in tribulations, knowing that tribulation produces perseverance; and perseverance, character; and character, hope. Now hope does not disappoint, because the love of God has been poured out in our hearts by the Holy Spirit who was given to us.

— ROMANS 5:3–5 NKJV

But the fruit of the Spirit is love, joy, peace, longsuffering, kindness, goodness, faithfulness, gentleness, self-control. Against such there is no law.

— GALATIANS 5:22–23 NKJV

He Would Minister in Galilee

Prophecy:

Nevertheless the gloom will not be upon her who is distressed, as when at first He lightly esteemed the land of Zebulun and the land of Naphtali, and afterward more heavily oppressed her, by the way of the sea, beyond the Jordan, in Galilee of the Gentiles. The people who walked in darkness have seen a great light; those who dwelt in the land of the shadow of death, upon them a light has shined.

– ISAIAH 9:1–2 NKJV

Fulfillment:

And leaving Nazareth he went and lived in Capernaum by the sea, in the territory of Zebulun and Naphtali, so that what was spoken by the prophet Isaiah might be fulfilled: "The land of Zebulun and the land of Naphtali, the way of the sea, beyond the Jordan, Galilee of the Gentiles—the people dwelling in darkness have seen a great light, and for those dwelling in the region and shadow of death, on them a light has dawned."

– MATTHEW 4:13–16 ESV

20

Enjoying Life

My Dear Friend,

I take great joy when I see My brothers and sisters enjoying the salvation that I purchased for them. Life is not meant to be lived in solemnity and seriousness all the time. I created this world for you to enjoy and take pleasure in.

I want you to know it is perfectly acceptable for you to have hobbies, spend time with friends and family, and find joy in the little things in life. I created you with unique passions and interests, and I want you to embrace them and use them to glorify Me. Whether it is through painting, music, sports, or any other pursuit, I want you to enjoy the talents and gifts I have given you.

I understand that sometimes the weight of your responsibilities and the challenges of life can press on you, making it difficult to enjoy your life. Even still, I want to remind you that I am always with you and that I will give you the strength, provision, and energy you need to fulfill your responsibilities and still have the time and resources for leisure.

I also want to remind you that you have been saved by grace and not by works, so there is no need to feel guilty for taking time to enjoy life and have fun. Your salvation is secure in Me, and I want you to live your life to the fullest. I came to the earth so you could have life and enjoy that life to the fullest. Your walk on this earth need not be a walk of mere survival. Learn to enjoy the journey with Me. Walk through your life with Me. In the tough moments, come to Me, and we can talk things out. When things are going well, come to Me, and I'll rejoice with you. Think of all the places we can visit together, all the beautiful moments we can share together in life!

So, go out and enjoy the life I have given you. Spend time with your loved ones, pursue your passions, and find joy in the simple things. I will be with you every step of the way, and I will be smiling with joy as I see you enjoying your salvation.

With love and blessings,

Jesus

(Psalm 147:11; Psalm 35:27; Ecclesiastes 8:15; Psalm 34:8; Psalm 118:24; Proverbs 17:22; Psalm 16:11; Proverbs 15:13; Romans 12:12; Psalm 100:1–2; Psalm 144:15; 1 Timothy 4:4–5; James 1:17; 1 Thessalonians 5:16; Philippians 4:4; John 15:11)

Scriptures on Enjoying Life————————————

"The thief comes only in order to steal and kill and destroy. I came that they may have and enjoy life, and have it in abundance (to the full, till it overflows)."

— JOHN 10:10 AMPC

And also that every man should eat and drink, and enjoy the good of all his labour, it is the gift of God.

— ECCLESIASTES 3:13 KJV

O taste and see that the LORD is good: blessed is the man that trusteth in him.

— PSALM 34:8 KJV

Every good gift and every perfect gift is from above, and cometh down from the Father of lights, with whom is no variableness, neither shadow of turning.

— JAMES 1:17 KJV

Charge them that are rich in this world, that they be not highminded, nor trust in uncertain riches, but in the living God, who giveth us richly all things to enjoy.

— 1 TIMOTHY 6:17 KJV

Delight thyself also in the LORD, and he shall give thee the desires of thine heart.

— PSALM 37:4 KJV

Wherefore do ye spend money for that which is not bread? and your labour for that which satisfieth not? hearken diligently unto me, and eat ye that which is good, and let your soul delight itself in fatness.

— ISAIAH 55:2 KJV

Not that I speak in respect of want: for I have learned, in whatsoever state I am, therewith to be content.

— PHILIPPIANS 4:11 KJV

He Would Speak in Parables

Prophecy:

My people, hear my teaching; listen to the words of my mouth. I will open my mouth with a parable; I will utter hidden things, things from of old.

– Psalm 78:1–2 NIV

Fulfilled:

Jesus spoke all these things to the crowd in parables; he did not say anything to them without using a parable. So was fulfilled what was spoken through the prophet: "I will open my mouth in parables, I will utter things hidden since the creation of the world."

– Matthew 13:34–35 NIV

21

Victory

Dearest Friend,

Through My death and resurrection, you have been given the opportunity to live a victorious life, free from the bondage of sin and death. Within you resides My indomitable, overcoming Spirit. I have made you more than a conqueror. I have made you triumphant—always! I never said you wouldn't have an opponent in this world, though. I have warned you that in this life, you will have trials, tests, and even suffering that you must face.

Yes, the midnight hour comes to all. You are not immune because you are Mine. But no matter how dark it may look or feel, you have My word that the light of the dawn will most certainly come. I know this because I am the Light that comes forth at dawn! I am the Hope of tomorrow. I am the Truth that shines bright on the way you should go.

Through faith and patience, you will see the manifestation of My goodness in your life. Do not be swayed by the lies of the enemy, who wants nothing more than to see you defeated and in despair. Instead, stand firm in your faith and trust in Me. Speak the truth of My Word over your life and resist the enemy with the authority I have given you.

When the obstacles in your life look large and immovable, then shout for joy, knowing how spectacular it will be when I bring them down. When the night seems so dark that you can't seem to see anything at all, rejoice all the louder, knowing that My light within you is about to shine brightly for all to see for miles around.

When the way is not clear, then come to Me. I am the way, and I will guide you and give you wisdom on how to proceed. The enemy of your soul will seek to confuse, discourage, and condemn you. Do not let him succeed in doing so. I have forgiven your past. Forge onward and fight the good fight of faith.

Rejoice in the victory that has already been won for you and let My joy and peace flow into every aspect of your life. You are My beloved, and I have called you to live a victorious life. So, arise and walk in the freedom and power I have given you. Do not be defeated, but be victorious in all things.

I am with you always,

Jesus

(2 Corinthians 2:14; Romans 8:37; 1 John 5:4; Psalm 44:4; Psalm 60:12; Psalm 20:6; 2 Chronicles 20:17; Revelation 12:11; Isaiah 54:17; Romans 8:31; 2 Timothy 4:7–8; 1 John 4:4; Ephesians 6:10–18; John 16:33; Colossians 2:15)

Scriptures on Victorious Living————————

For whatever is born of God overcomes the world. And this is the victory that has overcome the world—our faith.

— 1 JOHN 5:4 NKJV

Now thanks be unto God, which always causeth us to triumph in Christ, and maketh manifest the savour of his knowledge by us in every place.

— 2 CORINTHIANS 2:14 KJV

Therefore, since we are surrounded by such a great cloud of witnesses, let us throw off everything that hinders and the sin that so easily entangles. And let us run with perseverance the race marked out for us, fixing our eyes on Jesus, the pioneer and perfecter of faith. For the joy set before him he endured the cross, scorning its shame, and sat down at the right hand of the throne of God.

— HEBREWS 12:1–2 NIV

But thanks be to God! He gives us the victory through our Lord Jesus Christ.

— 1 CORINTHIANS 15:57 NIV

For God has not given us a spirit of fear, but of power and of love and of a sound mind.

— 2 TIMOTHY 1:7 NKJV

I have fought the good fight, I have finished the race, I have kept the faith.

— 2 TIMOTHY 4:7 NKJV

He Is the Great "I AM"

Prophecy:

God said to Moses, "I AM WHO I AM."

– Exodus 3:14 ESV

Fulfilled:

Jesus said to them, "Truly, truly, I say to you, before Abraham was, I am."

– John 8:58 ESV

22

Healing

Dear Child,

I come to you today as your Healer, the One who has the power to heal your physical ailments, your emotional wounds, and your spiritual brokenness. I know that you may be struggling with sickness, pain, and suffering, and I want you to know I am here to bring you comfort and healing.

I am the Son of God, and through My death and resurrection, I have conquered sin and death. This means I have the power to heal all that is broken in your life. I am the One who can restore your health, mend your relationships, and bring peace to your soul.

The answer to receiving My healing touch is simple: It comes through faith. Believe that I can heal you and that I want to heal you. And when you pray, ask Me to heal you, and believe that I will.

I know skepticism and doubt of My healing power are prevalent in the earth. Many say things like:

If Jesus is really the Healer, why doesn't He heal everyone? Why hasn't He healed me yet? Why are people born sick?

These, and a myriad of other questions, are often presented. You need to remember, though, that you can't always see the whole picture. You can only see things as clearly as you could if you were looking into a room through dimly lit glass. I urge you to get your eyes off of others and their situations of healing or death, and instead, fix your eyes on Me and My Word. Decide for yourself whether you will believe the words I have spoken or not. If you come to Me and talk to Me, in time I will reveal some things to you. You must come to Me not haughtily or demanding—I don't take kindly to the prideful—but if you'll fellowship with Me in sincerity and truth, I will provide clarity and peace for the questions that arise.

So, my dear friend, do not lose faith. Believe in My power to heal and My love for you. And when you pray, ask Me to heal you and believe that I will. As I am the true Healer, I will always be here to heal you, no matter what your circumstances. I love you, and I always will.

With My love and blessings,

Jesus

(Exodus 15:26; Psalm 103:2–3; Psalm 147:3; Isaiah 53:5; Matthew 9:35; Luke 4:18; 1 Peter 2:24; Matthew 4:23–24; Matthew 8:16–17; Matthew 9:35; Matthew 14:14; Acts 10:38; Luke 6:19; Luke 9:11; Acts 9:34; Luke 4:40; Mark 5:34; Acts 5:16; Luke 13:12; Matthew 15:30–31; Mark 10:52; Jeremiah 17:14)

Scriptures on Healing

My son, attend to my words; consent and submit to my sayings. Let them not depart from your sight; keep them in the center of your heart. For they are life to those who find them, healing and health to all their flesh.

– Proverbs 4:20–22 AMPC

He forgives all my sins and heals all my diseases. He redeems me from death and crowns me with love and tender mercies.

– Psalm 103:3–4 NLT

He heals the brokenhearted and binds up their wounds [curing their pains and their sorrows].

– Psalm 147:3 AMPC

Confess your sins to each other and pray for each other so that you may be healed. The earnest prayer of a righteous person has great power and produces wonderful results.

– James 5:16 NLT

He personally carried our sins in His body on the cross [willingly offering Himself on it, as on an altar of sacrifice], so that we might die to sin [becoming immune from the penalty and power of sin] and live for righteousness; for by His wounds you [who believe] have been healed.

– 1 Peter 2:24 AMP

But for you who fear my name, the Sun of Righteousness will rise with healing in his wings. And you will go free, leaping with joy like calves let out to pasture.

– Malachi 4:2 NLT

He himself bore our sins in his body on the cross, so that we might die to sins and live for righteousness; by his wounds you have been healed.

– 1 Peter 2:24 NIV

He said to her, "Daughter, your faith has healed you. Go in peace and be freed from your suffering."

– Mark 5:34 NIV

He Would Speak the Words of God

Prophecy:

"I will raise up for them a prophet like you from among their brothers. And I will put my words in his mouth, and he shall speak to them all that I command him."

– DEUTERONOMY 18:18 ESV

Fulfilled:

"For I have not spoken of myself; but the Father which sent me, he gave me a commandment, what I should say, and what I should speak. And I know that his commandment is life everlasting: whatsoever I speak therefore, even as the Father said unto me, so I speak."

– JOHN 12:49–50 KJV

23

Peace

My Beloved,

There is a tranquil state of existence you can enjoy. There is a spiritual force that can quiet all the questions and burning issues that arise in your heart and mind. It is My peace. When I left this world, I left My peace for you. My peace is not the same kind of peace with which the world is familiar. This world strives after and longs for something that I give to you freely.

My peace is not simply the absence of problems or conflict. Rather, My peace is tailor-made to help you thrive in the middle of problems and conflicts. My peace cannot be obtained through vacation time, extra sleep, or a day at the spa. My peace only comes through My presence.

My peace is not found in a trance or meditative state in which you are ignorant of the happenings around you. Instead, you can be fully aware of what is going on around you and remain unmoved due to your confident trust in Me. It doesn't make sense to the onlooker. They won't know how you can be at peace, and they won't understand it. It surpasses human reasoning because My peace is not born in the natural realm.

You can experience this peace by making Me the foundation of your life. When you place your trust in Me and make Me the center of your thoughts and actions, you will find that My peace begins to permeate every aspect of your life. This does not mean that your problems and difficulties will disappear, but rather, that you will have the strength and the perspective to face them with hope and confidence.

You can experience My peace daily by fixing your gaze on Me and spending time in quiet reflection and contemplation of My ways. Take time each day to talk to Me, listen for My voice, and meditate on My Word. As you do this, you will find that My peace begins to fill your heart and your mind, and that you are better able to navigate the challenges of life with grace and wisdom.

I also want to remind you that My peace is not just for you, but also for those around you. I have called you to be a peacemaker, an agent of My peace to your friends and family. As you share My love and My message of peace with others, you will be a shining light in a dark world, a powerful witness to My presence and power.

With love and blessings,

Jesus, your Prince of Peace

(Philippians 4:6–7; Colossians 3:15–17; John 14:27; Isaiah 48:22; Isaiah 57:21; Psalm 29:11; Isaiah 26:3; Romans 15:13; Matthew 5:9; 2 Thessalonians 3:16; Psalm 34:14; James 3:17–18; Isaiah 9:6; Psalm 85:8; Matthew 7:24–29; Hebrews 12:14; Matthew 5:23–24)

Scriptures on Peace ————————————————

And let the peace (soul harmony which comes) from Christ rule (act as umpire continually) in your hearts [deciding and settling with finality all questions that arise in your minds, in that peaceful state] to which as [members of Christ's] one body you were also called [to live]. And be thankful (appreciative), [giving praise to God always].

— COLOSSIANS 3:15 AMPC

"Peace I leave with you; my peace I give you. I do not give to you as the world gives. Do not let your hearts be troubled and do not be afraid."

— JOHN 14:27 NIV

You will keep in perfect peace those whose minds are steadfast, because they trust in you.

— ISAIAH 26:3 NIV

"I have told you these things, so that in me you may have peace. In this world you will have trouble. But take heart! I have overcome the world."

— JOHN 16:33 NIV

And the peace of God, which transcends all understanding, will guard your hearts and your minds in Christ Jesus.

— PHILIPPIANS 4:7 NIV

"Blessed are the peacemakers, for they will be called children of God."

— MATTHEW 5:9 NIV

He Would Be the Healer

Prophecy:

Then the eyes of the blind shall be opened, and the ears of the deaf shall be unstopped. Then shall the lame man leap as an hart, and the tongue of the dumb sing: for in the wilderness shall waters break out, and streams in the desert.

– Isaiah 35:5–6 KJV

Fulfilled:

"The blind receive their sight, and the lame walk, the lepers are cleansed, and the deaf hear, the dead are raised up, and the poor have the gospel preached to them."

– Matthew 11:5 KJV

24

Courage

My Dear Friend,

I am writing to you today to encourage you to be courageous in your everyday life. I know the world can be a difficult place, and there are many challenges you face on a daily basis. But I want you to know you are not alone. You have the strength and the ability to overcome any obstacle that comes your way.

As My follower, you are called to be a light to the world, to let My light, My love, and My compassion shine through you to the world around you. Be courageous as My voice of hope, healing, and comfort to those you encounter who are discouraged and hurting.

Courage is not the absence of fear, but the ability to act in spite of it. You will experience fear, doubt, and uncertainty in this world, but you must not let it stop you from doing what is right. Instead, use it as a motivator to push forward and make a difference in the world.

I encourage you to be courageous in your relationships. It takes courage to love others unconditionally, to forgive those who have hurt you, and to stand by those who are going through difficult times. In a world where people often look out for their own interests, it takes courage to put others first.

Be courageous enough to stand up for Me, to speak your mind and heart, knowing that I have your back. When necessary, don't be afraid to go against the crowd for My name's sake. It is easy to be swayed by the opinions of others, but true courage comes from standing firm in your convictions born of faith and love.

Lastly, I want to remind you that I am always with you, and that you can find strength and courage in My love. When you are feeling weak or uncertain, turn to Me in prayer and know I am there to guide and support you.

In conclusion, My dear family, I encourage you to be courageous in your everyday life. Stand up for what is right, love and forgive others, and always remember that I am with you. Together, we can make a difference in the world, bringing hope and light to those who need it most.

With love and blessings,

Jesus

(Joshua 1:9; Deuteronomy 31:6; Psalm 27:14; 1 Corinthians 16:13; 2 Timothy 1:7; Isaiah 41:10; Psalm 31:24; 1 Chronicles 28:20; Isaiah 43:2; 1 Samuel 17:47; Mark 8:38; Acts 4:13; 2 Timothy 1:8; Romans 1:16; Ephesians 6:13; Matthew 5:14–16; 2 Corinthians 1:3–4; Isaiah 58:10; Proverbs 28:1; Ephesians 3:12; Hebrews 4:16; 2 Corinthians 3:12; Acts 14:3; Proverbs 10:9; Hebrews 10:35–36)

Scriptures on Courage ———————————

"Be strong and courageous, be not afraid nor dismayed for the king of Assyria, nor for all the multitude that is with him: for there be more with us than with him: With him is an arm of flesh; but with us is the LORD our God to help us, and to fight our battles. And the people rested themselves upon the words of Hezekiah king of Judah."

— 2 CHRONICLES 32:7–8 KJV

For God has not given us a spirit of fear, but of power and of love and of a sound mind.

— 2 TIMOTHY 1:7 NKJV

"Do not fear, for I am with you; do not be dismayed, for I am your God. I will strengthen you and help you; I will uphold you with my righteous right hand."

— ISAIAH 41:10 NIV

The LORD is my strength and my shield; my heart trusts in him, and he helps me. My heart leaps for joy, and with my song I praise him.

— PSALM 28:7 NIV

Be on your guard; stand firm in the faith; be courageous; be strong.

— 1 CORINTHIANS 16:13 NIV

For the Spirit God gave us does not make us timid, but gives us power, love and self-discipline.

— 2 TIMOTHY 1:7 NIV

And David said to his son Solomon, "Be strong and of good courage, and do it; do not fear nor be dismayed, for the LORD God— my God—will be with you. He will not leave you nor forsake you, until you have finished all the work for the service of the house of the LORD."

— 1 CHRONICLES 28:20 NKJV

He Would Be Zealous for the Lord's House

Prophecy:

For zeal for your house has consumed me, and the reproaches of those who reproach you have fallen on me.

— PSALM 69:9 ESV

Fulfilled:

The Passover of the Jews was at hand, and Jesus went up to Jerusalem. In the temple he found those who were selling oxen and sheep and pigeons, and the money-changers sitting there. And making a whip of cords, he drove them all out of the temple, with the sheep and oxen. And he poured out the coins of the money-changers and overturned their tables. And he told those who sold the pigeons, "Take these things away; do not make my Father's house a house of trade." His disciples remembered that it was written, "Zeal for your house will consume me."

— JOHN 2:13–17 ESV

25

Anxiety and Worry

Dearest Child,

I know life can be difficult, and there are many things that can tempt you to worry and feel anxious. I want you to know that just as the world, with all its sin and turmoil, can tempt you to give in to fear, My Word invites you to a banquet of faith. Feelings of fear, worry, and anxiety are bound to come, but experiencing these feelings and having those thoughts are not what is harming you; it's treating these things as if they belong.

Worry and anxiety are not from Me, but rather, they are from the enemy. He wants to steal your peace and joy, but I have overcome him, and I have given you the authority to do the same. Anxiety and worry put an emphasis on the strength of your foe and the weakness lurking in yourself. When anxious and worried feelings attempt to overwhelm you, it is critical that you resist them and come straight to Me. The primary root of these feelings and thoughts is doubt. Feed on My Word, and not on the doubt that your situation breeds. Doubt poisons your soul, but faith purifies your soul like a blade in fire. Come to Me; I don't expect you to fight alone, but I do expect you to fight. Remember that I have already overcome the world and all its troubles, so you can trust in Me to guide and strengthen you through any difficulties that may come your way.

I encourage you to practice gratitude and focus on the blessings in your life. When worries and anxieties try to creep in, remind yourself of all the good things I have given you and the love I have for you. This will help to shift your perspective and bring peace to your heart.

I gave you a charge in My Word: to cast all your cares upon Me. I did this because I care for you. Worry does not fix the problem—it only wastes today's strength on tomorrow's problems. Each day has enough trouble of its own; don't add to them with tomorrow's load. Look to Me to take care of today's challenges instead.

When it comes to anxiety, I know it can be very debilitating. Don't open the door to anxiety, not even an inch. The moment it starts to take hold of your thoughts and emotions, slam the door on it and begin to make your thanksgiving and requests known to Me in prayer. If you are in a public setting, then do it silently in your heart or under your breath. I promise you that My peace, which transcends all understanding, will guard your heart and your mind against that anxiety.

Dear child, I know it can feel like sticky paper when you are trying to cast your cares on Me. One moment you think you have thrown your cares away, just to look down and realize they are stuck to your other hand. You may have to cast the same cares on Me multiple times, but keep doing so, and I promise I'll take care of them for you.

Let go of your worries, and trust in Me. I love you, and I will take care of you.

In My love,

Jesus

(John 16:33; Matthew 6:25–27; Romans 10:17; 1 Peter 5:8; 1 John 4:4; James 1:6; 1 Peter 1:7; Matthew 11:28; 1 Thessalonians 5:18; 1 Peter 5:7; Matthew 6:34; Philippians 4:6–7; Proverbs 3:5–6; Psalm 55:22; Hebrews 11:1; Isaiah 41:10; 2 Timothy 1:7; Mark 11:23; James 1:3; Psalm 32:8; Psalm 136:1; Proverbs 12:25; Psalm 56:3)

Scriptures on Anxiety and Worry —————————————

But when I am afraid, I will put my trust in you. I praise God for what he has promised. I trust in God, so why should I be afraid? What can mere mortals do to me?

– PSALM 56:3–4 NLT

"So do not worry, saying, 'What shall we eat?' or 'What shall we drink?' or 'What shall we wear?' For the pagans run after all these things, and your heavenly Father knows that you need them. But seek first his kingdom and his righteousness, and all these things will be given to you as well. Therefore do not worry about tomorrow, for tomorrow will worry about itself. Each day has enough trouble of its own."

– MATTHEW 6:31–34 NIV

Do not be anxious about anything, but in every situation, by prayer and petition, with thanksgiving, present your requests to God.

– PHILIPPIANS 4:6 NIV

Cast all your anxiety on him because he cares for you.

– 1 PETER 5:7 NIV

Cast your burden on the LORD, and he will sustain you; he will never permit the righteous to be moved.

– PSALM 55:22 ESV

Unless the LORD had been my help, my soul would soon have settled in silence. If I say, "My foot slips," Your mercy, O LORD, will hold me up. In the multitude of my anxieties within me, Your comforts delight my soul.

– PSALM 94:17–19 NKJV

He Would Declare Things Not Yet Done

Prophecy:

"Remember the former things, those of long ago; I am God, and there is no other; I am God, and there is none like me. I make known the end from the beginning, from ancient times, what is still to come. I say, 'My purpose will stand, and I will do all that I please.'"

— ISAIAH 46:9–10 NIV

Fulfilled:

I am telling you this now, before it takes place, that when it does take place you may believe that I am he.

— JOHN 13:19 ESV

26

Fear Not

Dear Child,

I come to you today to remind you there is no need to fear, for I am with you always. I understand the world can be a difficult and uncertain place, and that fear can grip your heart and your mind if you are mindful of the wrong things. But I want to assure you that you are never alone, that I am always here to guide you and protect you.

It is natural to feel fear in times of trouble, but I want you to remember that fear is not from Me. Just because your hands are shaking and your knees feel weak does not mean the fight is lost for you. Force strength back into your hands and knees, straighten your back, and call your thoughts into submission. I am the Prince of Peace, and I bring comfort and hope to all who call on My name. What are you mindful of when fear grips you? It's certainly not of Me or the words I've spoken to you. Perfect love casts out all fear, My beloved. Is there a more perfect love than that of the Father? Be mindful of Him, and your fear will dissipate. It's a battle, and the fear will look for a foothold wherever it can if you let it. Don't let it.

I understand that many things tempt you to fear, be it illness, poverty, persecution, or even death. But I have overcome all these challenges, and in Me, you, too, can find the strength to triumph. I am the resurrection and the life; I have defeated death itself and reside within you. What obstacle stands in your path that you trust more in its potential to harm you than in My love for you?

When you feel afraid, remember Our love for you. Turn to the Father in prayer, pour out your heart to Him, and ask for help and guidance. The peace that passes all understanding will garrison your heart against the threats of the world. All who turn to the Father as their refuge and strength will never be disappointed.

Don't let fear run free in your life; it is your enemy. It can prevent you from doing the things you are called to do. It can hold you back from sharing the Good News of My love with others, from reaching out to those in need, and from standing up for what is right. So, I urge you to be strong and courageous, to trust in Me and step out in faith, knowing that I have your back. Do not be afraid, for I am the God who makes the impossible possible. I can do more than you can ever ask or imagine.

Remember that I am the Light of the world, and that in Me, there is no darkness at all. I am the One who drives away all shadows and fears, and I am the One who brings hope and peace to all who call on My name.

Do not be afraid, dear child, for I am with you always. I love you, and I will never leave you, nor forsake you.

Yours always,

Jesus

(Isaiah 41:10; John 16:33; Matthew 28:20; 2 Timothy 1:7; Isaiah 9:6; 1 John 4:18; John 11:25; Philippians 4:6–7; Psalm 46:1; Psalm 34:4; Joshua 1:9; Luke 1:37; John 8:12; Hebrews 13:5)

Scriptures on Fear —————————————————————

Strengthen the weak hands, and make firm the feeble knees. Say to those who are fearful-hearted, "Be strong, do not fear! Behold, your God will come with vengeance, with the recompense of God; He will come and save you."

— Isaiah 35:3–4 NKJV

"Be strong and courageous. Do not be afraid or terrified because of them, for the Lord your God goes with you; he will never leave you nor forsake you."

— Deuteronomy 31:6 NIV

I will not fear though tens of thousands assail me on every side.

— Psalm 3:6 NIV

The Lord is my light and my salvation—so why should I be afraid? The Lord is my fortress, protecting me from danger, so why should I tremble? When evil people come to devour me, when my enemies and foes attack me, they will stumble and fall. Though a mighty army surrounds me, my heart will not be afraid. Even if I am attacked, I will remain confident. The one thing I ask of the Lord—the thing I seek most—is to live in the house of the Lord all the days of my life, delighting in the Lord's perfections and meditating in his Temple. For he will conceal me there when troubles come; he will hide me in his sanctuary. He will place me out of reach on a high rock. Then I will hold my head high above my enemies who surround me. At his sanctuary I will offer sacrifices with shouts of joy, singing and praising the Lord with music.

— Psalm 27:1–6 NLT

Even though I walk through the darkest valley, I will fear no evil, for you are with me.

— Psalm 23:4 NIV

The Lord is on my side; I will not fear. What can man do to me?

— Psalm 118:6 NKJV

For God has not given us a spirit of fear, but of power and of love and of a sound mind.

— 2 Timothy 1:7 NKJV

He Would Send the Spirit of God

Prophecy:

"For I will pour water on the thirsty land, and streams on the dry ground; I will pour my Spirit upon your offspring, and my blessing on your descendants."

— Isaiah 44:3 ESV

Fulfilled:

Nevertheless, I tell you the truth: it is to your advantage that I go away, for if I do not go away, the Helper will not come to you. But if I go, I will send him to you.

— John 16:7 ESV

27

Offense

Dearest Friend,

You are not defined by the opinions or actions of others. It is easy to become offended when someone speaks against you or does something you perceive as hurtful. However, I urge you to remember that their words or actions do not define you. These are only a reflection of their own thoughts and feelings, often misguided because of their own pain and hurt. Their harsh treatment of you does not change who you truly are.

Remember that the approval of others is not necessary for your happiness or fulfillment. You were created with a unique purpose and destiny, and you are not meant to fit into the mold of what others expect or want you to be. It is essential that you seek to understand and fulfill your own purpose, given by Me, rather than accepting the limitations placed on you by others.

I understand it can be difficult to let go of the need for the approval of others. Society often teaches people that to be happy, they must be accepted and valued by those around them. But I assure you, true joy and fulfillment come from living in alignment with My Word. When you seek My approval instead of the world's acceptance, then you will find true peace and contentment.

When you are constantly seeking the approval of others, then you will also find yourself constantly offended. Do not give away to others, so recklessly, the power to harm you. When you make Me the source of your identity and confidence, then you remove the ability of others to harm you through their harsh treatment of you. Your identity, self-worth, and confidence become untouchable.

However, this does not mean you should completely disregard those around you. Part of growing close to others is sharing with them a certain level of vulnerability. I have called you to love everyone—but not trust everyone. Trust only comes with time and a proven track record of faithfulness. So be patient before you trust, and be cautious with whom you share your dreams and heart.

If a person does lash out at you or hurts you, then extend grace and forgiveness to them. This does not mean you must continue to allow yourself to be mistreated, but it does mean you can release the anger and resentment that often accompany such an offense. When you can forgive, you are able to move forward and let go of the past, which will bring you greater freedom and peace.

So, I encourage you to let go of the need for the approval of others and to forgive those who have hurt you. It may be difficult, but it is essential for your own happiness and fulfillment. Remember that you are loved and valued, and you are not defined by the opinions or actions of others.

May you experience peace and joy as you seek My approval and let go of the need for the approval of others.

With love,

Jesus

(Psalm 139:14; Galatians 1:10; Romans 12:2; Ephesians 2:10; Psalm 119:105; Proverbs 29:25; 2 Corinthians 5:17; Proverbs 3:5–6; Colossians 3:13; Philippians 3:13–14; Zephaniah 3:17)

Scriptures on Offense————————————————

Whatever may be your task, work at it heartily (from the soul), as [something done] for the Lord and not for men, knowing [with all certainty] that it is from the Lord [and not from men] that you will receive the inheritance which is your [real] reward. [The One Whom] you are actually serving [is] the Lord Christ (the Messiah).
— COLOSSIANS 3:23–24 AMPC

Obviously, I'm not trying to win the approval of people, but of God. If pleasing people were my goal, I would not be Christ's servant.
— GALATIANS 1:10 NLT

An offended friend is harder to win back than a fortified city.
— PROVERBS 18:19 NLT

"Blessed is he who is not offended because of Me."
— MATTHEW 11:6 NKJV

It is to one's glory to overlook an offense.
— PROVERBS 19:11 NIV

But as we have been approved by God to be entrusted with the gospel, even so we speak, not as pleasing men, but God who tests our hearts.
— 1 THESSALONIANS 2:4 NKJV

It is better to trust in the LORD than to put confidence in man.
— PSALM 118:8 NKJV

"How can you believe, who receive honor from one another, and do not seek the honor that comes from the only God?"
— JOHN 5:44 NKJV

He Is the Only Savior

Prophecy:

"I, I am the LORD, and besides me there is no savior."

— ISAIAH 43:11 ESV

Fulfilled:

Jesus answered, "I am the way and the truth and the life. No one comes to the Father except through me."

— JOHN 14:6 NIV

28

Get Back Up

My Dear Friend,

Everyone falls at one point or another. I am not just referring to sin, though often sin will cause you to fall. There are many ways to stumble, whether it be through a failure or mistake, or as simple as an unexpected setback or a frustrating hindrance that has tripped you up. Regardless of the reason for your stumble, you must always remember you are not defined by your falls, but by your resilience and determination to get back up and keep going.

I understand it can be hard to find the motivation and willpower to get back up. I know it can be easy to get caught up in the negative thoughts and feelings that come with falling, but I want you to remember that faith is an act, and courage is not a feeling, but the triumph over them. When you feel most insecure, afraid, and weak, you can courageously get back up in faith and press on.

If you fall one hundred times, then get up one hundred times. If life puts your face where your feet were a few moments before, then grit your teeth and stand back up through the pain. You are an overcomer, so overcome your weakness. You are more than a conqueror, so conquer your trepidation. Take heart and be of good cheer. If your opponent presents an issue, know that I have already overcome it and can teach you how it is done.

Again, My friend, it is not the falling that signifies the end of a battle, but rather, it is your response to the blow that determines the outcome. Each time you fall and get back up, you become stronger and more resilient. And even though it may be difficult to see it at the time, you are becoming battle-worn and tested, your faith is being refined, and you are becoming a greater threat to the kingdom of darkness.

So, do not let temporary setbacks hold you back from living a fulfilling and meaningful life. Even though you may feel defeated in the moment, your story is not over yet. Keep your eyes fixed on Me and the plans I have for you, and know I am always working in your life for your good and for My glory.

With all My love,

Jesus

(Proverbs 24:16; Micah 7:8; Joshua 1:9; Psalm 37:23–24; 1 John 5:4; Romans 8:37; John 16:33; James 1:2–4; 1 Peter 1:6–7; Hebrews 12:2)

Scriptures on Getting Back Up

This is what the LORD says: "When people fall down, don't they get up again? When they discover they're on the wrong road, don't they turn back?"

— JEREMIAH 8:4 NLT

Though he fall, he shall not be utterly cast down; for the LORD upholds him with His hand.

— PSALM 37:24 NKJV

To him who is able to keep you from stumbling and to present you before his glorious presence without fault and with great joy.

— JUDE 1:24 NIV

For though the righteous fall seven times, they rise again.

— PROVERBS 24:16 NIV

Even youths grow tired and weary, and young men stumble and fall; but those who hope in the LORD will renew their strength. They will soar on wings like eagles; they will run and not grow weary, they will walk and not be faint.

— ISAIAH 40:30–31 NIV

Heaven Would Be Clothed in Black at His Humiliation

Prophecy:

"I clothe the heavens with blackness and make sackcloth their covering."

– Isaiah 50:3 ESV

Fulfilled:

It was now about the sixth hour, and there was darkness over the whole land until the ninth hour, while the sun's light failed. And the curtain of the temple was torn in two.

– Luke 23:44–45 ESV

29

Discouragement and Weariness

My Dear Friend,

I offer to you this day a light and easy load. I offer to you this hour a real rest for your soul. I offer you times of refreshing in My presence. The same Spirit that caused Me to rise from the dead will infuse your body with life. I offer you the ability to soar with a heavenly perspective, in freedom and truth, high above the difficulties of this world. I offer you the ability to run your race with endurance and patience without feeling the effects of weariness. I offer you the ability to walk slowly and confidently in My authority without fainting or faltering.

All you must do is hope in Me, trust in Me, and lean on Me.

When you are feeling discouraged, it is easy to lose sight of the hope you have in Me. When you are feeling weary, then the temptation to give up can become an enticing option. I knew ahead of time that you would face these issues. That's why I gave you the promises in My Word. You needn't carry on in your own strength. I have strength enough to spare.

You needn't carry anything I don't give you, and anything I do give you I also equip you to carry. I give you the grace to support the load, making it light and easy.

This world is full of burdens, but I am not. This world is full of stress, worries, fears, pressures, and problems, but I am not. So, if you feel wearied and discouraged in your situation, come to Me. Lay your load upon Me. Give Me your shame, your embarrassment, your guilt, your sin, your frustration, your pain, and all your sorrows. The punishment that was needed to obtain peace, I took. I have purchased peace and rest just for you. You needn't suffer, My beloved; come to Me.

Lastly, remember that you are not alone in this family. You have brothers and sisters on the earth with you who are also My sons and daughters. Don't be afraid to reach out to them. Together, with My strength and guidance, you can lift each other up and help each other through these difficult times. Remember, I have called you to be in community with one another, to share in each other's joys and sorrows, to bear each other's burdens, and to encourage one another in the faith.

With love,

Jesus

(Isaiah 54:4; Romans 10:11; Hebrews 10:22; 1 John 1:9; Psalm 37:7–8; Revelation 21:4; Isaiah 53:4; Matthew 11:30; Matthew 11:29; Romans 8:11; Isaiah 40:31; Hebrews 12:1; Luke 10:19; Proverbs 3:5–6; Philippians 4:13; 2 Corinthians 12:9; Isaiah 53:5; Galatians 6:2)

Scriptures on Discouragement and Weariness————

"This is my command—be strong and courageous! Do not be afraid or discouraged. For the LORD your God is with you wherever you go."

— JOSHUA 1:9 NLT

"Come to me, all you who are weary and burdened, and I will give you rest. Take my yoke upon you and learn from me, for I am gentle and humble in heart, and you will find rest for your souls. For my yoke is easy and my burden is light."

— MATTHEW 11:28–30 NIV

And let us not grow weary of doing good, for in due season we will reap, if we do not give up.

— GALATIANS 6:9 ESV

He gives strength to the weary and increases the power of the weak.

— ISAIAH 40:29 NIV

"You have persevered and have endured hardships for my name, and have not grown weary."

— REVELATION 2:3 NIV

But as for you, brethren, do not grow weary in doing good.

— 2 THESSALONIANS 3:13 NKJV

For I will [fully] satisfy the weary soul, and I will replenish every languishing and sorrowful person.

— JEREMIAH 31:25 AMPC

He Would Be Silent before His Accusers

Prophecy:

He was oppressed, and he was afflicted, yet he opened not his mouth; like a lamb that is led to the slaughter, and like a sheep that before its shearers is silent, so he opened not his mouth.

– Isaiah 53:7b ESV

Fulfilled:

But when he was accused by the chief priests and elders, he gave no answer. Then Pilate said to him, "Do you not hear how many things they testify against you?" But he gave him no answer, not even to a single charge, so that the governor was greatly amazed.

– Matthew 27:12–14 ESV

30

Confronting the Enemy

My Dear Believer,

I would not have you ignorant of the devil and his devices. It is imperative that you understand these things.

You have an enemy, one who kills, steals, and destroys; one who seeks to undermine your faith and lead you astray. This enemy is not flesh and blood, but it is the devil himself. He is a deceiver and a liar, and he will use any means necessary to turn you away from Me. He will try to tempt you with worldly desires and pleasures, and he will try to convince you that My teachings are too difficult or unrealistic to follow. He will try to make you doubt My love for you and My power to save you. Ultimately, Satan's goal is to separate you from Me.

Your enemy roams around looking for someone whom he *may* devour. Don't let him devour you. Satan is not all-powerful. He is a defeated enemy, and through My death and resurrection, I have given you the authority to resist him and overcome him. All he can do is tempt you to walk away from Me so that then you can be devoured.

Not everything that happens in life to you is part of My will. You have an enemy. I do not appreciate it when atrocious acts are attributed to Me instead of him. You must get this straight. How can you ever have faith and trust in Me if you can't even tell the difference between Me and a being who wants nothing more than your suffering? I have come so that you may have life and enjoy it. He has come to kill, steal, and destroy you. So, whose plan do you think the killing and destruction on the earth belongs to?

There is a very simple test you can use with anything in your life to determine whether it is from Me or the enemy. The test is this:

If it is good, it is from Me. If it is bad, then it is from the enemy.

It is really that simple. Does it kill something in your life? Does it steal something in your life? Does it destroy something in your life? If the answer is yes to any of these questions, then it is not from Me.

Lastly, it is important for you to understand that the voice of Satan is filled with deceit, doubt, and unbelief. He will attempt to confuse you or cause you to waver in your conviction. It is always easy to pick out his voice because it is the opposite of My voice. His voice will always bring to you doubt and unbelief. My voice is the voice of faith, and it is always simple. Doubt focuses on all the complexities of the issue, but faith focuses on Me and My ability to handle it.

Do not fear, My beloved. You may have an enemy, but you also have Me. Stand firm in your faith, stay close to Me, trust in Me, and resist the devil—then he will run in terror from you.

Sincerely,
Jesus

(2 Corinthians 2:11; John 10:10; Ephesians 6:12; James 1:13–14; James 4:7; Ephesians 4:27; James 1:17; 1 John 4:1; John 8:44; Romans 10:17; Romans 16:20; 1 Peter 5:8–9)

Scriptures on Confronting the Enemy ———————

Submit to God. Resist the devil and he will flee from you.

— JAMES 4:7 NKJV

"Behold, I have given you authority to tread on serpents and scorpions, and over all the power of the enemy, and nothing shall hurt you."

— LUKE 10:19 ESV

Be sober, be vigilant; because your adversary the devil walks about like a roaring lion, seeking whom he may devour.

— 1 PETER 5:8 NKJV

Nor give place to the devil.

— EPHESIANS 4:27 NKJV

For though we walk (live) in the flesh, we are not carrying on our warfare according to the flesh and using mere human weapons. For the weapons of our warfare are not physical [weapons of flesh and blood], but they are mighty before God for the overthrow and destruction of strongholds, [inasmuch as we] refute arguments and theories and reasonings and every proud and lofty thing that sets itself up against the [true] knowledge of God; and we lead every thought and purpose away captive into the obedience of Christ (the Messiah, the Anointed One).

— 2 CORINTHIANS 10:3–5 AMPC

Put on all of God's armor so that you will be able to stand firm against all strategies of the devil.

— EPHESIANS 6:11 NLT

The Spirit of the Lord Would Be upon Him

Prophecy:

"The Spirit of the Lord God is upon me; because the Lord hath anointed me to preach good tidings unto the meek; he hath sent me to bind up the brokenhearted, to proclaim liberty to the captives, and the opening of the prison to them that are bound; to proclaim the acceptable year of the Lord, and the day of vengeance of our God; to comfort all that mourn."

— Isaiah 61:1–2 KJV

Fulfillment:

"The Spirit of the Lord is upon me, because he hath anointed me to preach the gospel to the poor; he hath sent me to heal the brokenhearted, to preach deliverance to the captives, and recovering of sight to the blind, to set at liberty them that are bruised, to preach the acceptable year of the Lord. And he closed the book, and he gave it again to the minister, and sat down. And the eyes of all them that were in the synagogue were fastened on him. And he began to say unto them, This day is this scripture fulfilled in your ears."

— Luke 4:18–21 KJV

31

You Are Not Alone

My Beloved,

You are not alone. I will not leave you. In all your goings and comings throughout life, you will never have to part from Me. When you leave your home, I'm coming with you. When you get in the car, then I'm in the car with you. When you arrive at work, then I arrive at work with you. You greet many people throughout the day, saying hello and good-bye. You and I will never have this interaction. Even while you sleep, I am there, watching over you, ready to commune with you as you awaken. The closest to a greeting we will ever share is when you say, "good morning," as I share with you the wonders of the day I made especially for you, and when you say, "good night," as I watch over you and keep you in perfect peace as you sleep.

You are Mine, and I am yours. I have made a covenant with you, and we have a marriage unlike any that you've ever seen. There will never be a time when you are alone from now on. Call on Me, and I'll answer. I'll be with you in times of trouble. I'll be with you when there are tears and weeping. I will be with you when there are times of rejoicing and celebration. I know your likes and dislikes better than anyone else alive. Even as you read these words, I am preparing a place in heaven just for you that is as unique and special as you are.

Will you journey through life with Me? Will you be My hands and feet to the hurting, the broken, and the lost? Will you experience the abundance of life I have for you, spending each and every day in My presence? Will you speak to Me and walk with Me as Adam and Eve once did in the Garden?

I put on display, for all of creation to see, My love for you. I even put My very own Spirit inside you. Sure, there will be storms. I am not just the One who delivers you out of storms; I'm also the One who will walk through the storm with you. If you're in a den of lions, I'll shut their mouths. If you are in a fiery furnace, I'll meet you right there in the middle of it. So often My disciples get into trouble; still I am there to get them out.

You are not alone.

I love you,

Jesus

(Hebrews 13:5; Psalm 121:8; Joshua 1:9; Psalm 4:8; Jeremiah 31:33; Psalm 34:18; 2 Corinthians 1:4; John 14:2; Micah 6:8; 1 Corinthians 6:19; Mark 4:39; Daniel 6:22; Daniel 3:25; Matthew 28:20; Isaiah 41:10; Psalm 23:4; Zephaniah 3:17; Psalm 139:7–10; Matthew 1:23; Joshua 1:5; Romans 8:38–39; Deuteronomy 20:4; Haggai 2:5; Isaiah 43:2)

Scriptures on Feeling Alone —————————————————

Yes, furthermore, I count everything as loss compared to the possession of the priceless privilege (the overwhelming preciousness, the surpassing worth, and supreme advantage) of knowing Christ Jesus my Lord and of progressively becoming more deeply and intimately acquainted with Him [of perceiving and recognizing and understanding Him more fully and clearly]. For His sake I have lost everything and consider it all to be mere rubbish (refuse, dregs), in order that I may win (gain) Christ (the Anointed One).

— PHILIPPIANS 3:8 AMPC

In conclusion, be strong in the Lord [be empowered through your union with Him]; draw your strength from Him [that strength which His boundless might provides].

— EPHESIANS 6:10 AMPC

"Have I not commanded you? Be strong and courageous! Do not be terrified or dismayed (intimidated), for the LORD your God is with you wherever you go."

— JOSHUA 1:9 AMP

"Do not fear [anything], for I am with you; do not be afraid, for I am your God. I will strengthen you, be assured I will help you; I will certainly take hold of you with My righteous right hand [a hand of justice, of power, of victory, of salvation]."

— ISAIAH 41:10 AMP

"For He [God] Himself has said, I will not in any way fail you nor give you up nor leave you without support. [I will] not, [I will] not, [I will] not in any degree leave you helpless nor forsake nor let you down (relax My hold on you)! [Assuredly not]!"

— HEBREWS 13:5 AMPC

"I will not leave you as orphans; I will come to you."

— JOHN 14:18 NIV

For this God is our God for ever and ever; he will be our guide even to the end.

— PSALM 48:14 NIV

The Retelling:
I Was There

I was there at the beginning—before there was man, before there was an earth, before there was rebellion. I was there when the archangel Lucifer tested his faith and mettle against My Father. I was there when their words clashed with each other, and Satan fell like lightning in defeat. I was there when a third of the angels underneath the archangel's charge defected with him. I was there when Our Father decided He would repopulate heaven's lost worshipers with a different, much more, replacement; I was there as He decided to make a being in Our image, who would begin the line of true worshipers, who would worship Him in spirit and in truth. Simply put, I was there when Our Father decided to have kids. Then it was time to create a place for His children, a universe to put the place in, and a realm for which these things could all operate in harmony for the kids. This would be a place where they could have the ability of choice and free governance over the realm. I was there, working in tandem with Him, as the dream of His heart was spoken into fruition, bathing the new realm in light. I was there as His Spirit hovered over the face of the deep—as the division between waters, lands, heavens, seasons, darkness, and light was set. I was there as He measured the waters in the palms of His hands—as He made careful measurements of the heavens and the mountains, and even stilled the dust to be measured. I was there as color vibrantly shown forth on the face of the earth with every sort of fruit and vegetation. I was there as We hung the stars, the moon, and the sun in the sky. I was there as creatures of land, sea, and sky were given unique purpose and designs. Now, it was finally time. After five days of attentive preparation, it was time for the grand finale. The realm, the universe, the world, and the Garden had been created and made ready; all that was missing was the one who would govern them. I'll never forget that day, as the Father called Me and His Holy Spirit into His presence and said, "Let Us make man in Our own image and give him the dominion over all that We have done in this realm." So man was formed. The replacement to what was lost—a spirit, a soul, and a body—made in Our image, given authority and dominion, now roamed no longer in Our thoughts alone, but now in the world We had created for him.

I was there, My dear friend, as We walked with Adam and Eve in the cool of the morning. I was there as Our intimacy grew, as questions were answered, and as the naming of animals was completed. It was a special time. Sadly, I was also there as the shame of sin had wrought its sinister devices on My once beautiful and wonderful friends. They had taken the word of a serpent over Mine, and they chose to partake of the only thing off-limits to them. The pain it caused was deep both for them and for Us. It was a day that caused a catastrophic downward spiral of sin and death on the earth. The first casualty was the deadliest—Our intimacy. We could not be partnered with sin and rebellion; it is against Our very nature and of holiness. It's difficult to describe the pain it caused for one who loves as deeply as the Father does. Justice had to be dealt out, and the downward spiral continued through labor, exile, a divorce of authority and dominion, and an eventual physical death. I was there, surely I tell you, I was there.

Happily, however, I was also there when We decided that We would not leave humanity to the fate they had chosen for themselves. Our Father, the Master Planner, had laid a path of assistance—a path of care, a path of honor, a path of redemption—a path that We alone could walk, but a path that they must choose.

I was there as Abel took his very best and laid it before the Lord as a sacrifice, and then I heard his innocent blood cry out as it was unjustly spilled by his brother. I was there as Enoch, who had only heard stories from his forefathers and -mothers about how they had walked with God, thought it not impossible, and deemed God good enough for him to walk with one such as himself. He walks with God still. I was there as sin infested every corner of the world save one heart—Noah's heart. I was there as Noah built the ark out of faith and obedience in the face of ridicule and disgrace. I was there as it rained for forty days and forty nights. I was there when a rainbow was formed, a promise was given, and a new beginning for mankind commenced. I was there as autonomy was coveted, and rebellion under the guise of unity was formed among all peoples in the construction of a tower. I was there as We scattered these people to the four winds for their vanity.

Though time and time again, it seemed as though man would choose their own demise, still there existed hope, light, and goodness.

Much like Noah was found, I was there as another was found whose faith caught the eye of Our Father. I was there when Abraham deemed Us faithful and good, and I was there when he bet the life of his only begotten son on that fact. I was there when the Father made a covenant with Abraham. I bore witness, while Abraham slept, to the Father walking through the blood twice, shouldering the weight of commitment. I watched over him and his seed as the blessing and covenant made a way for them in a world of sin and rebellion. I took note of the pleasure it brought the Father, seeing His covenanted partners prospering. I couldn't help but smile Myself as faith grew in the hearts and lips of Abraham's descendants. Many forget that his son, Isaac, was willing and obedient to his father—willing to make himself a sacrifice. The faith and blessing of Abraham would pass to Isaac and then to Jacob, not Esau. Isaac might have been deceived by the ruse that Jacob and his mother had performed, but I was not. Where many would have considered it an impertinence,

I appreciated the tenacious spirit of a young man who placed the highest value on My things while his brother despised them. I was there as the seed of the tribes first took root. I was there as the family betrayal thrust Joseph into the heart of foreign cruelty. Joseph honored the Father, and I blessed the work of his hands. I was with him in times of trouble. He did not falter. He did not fade. He fled from temptation, and he endured captivity with a cheerful heart. Through him, I protected the covenant, his family, and the land. I did not leave as the wine turned sour in Egypt. I remember the cries of Our people for deliverance. I was there as the bush burned with My holy fire. I was there as the exodus began in the heart of Moses. I was there as man refused the Most High. I was there when the Nile ran red. They did not relent. I heard the ceaseless croaking that supplanted the stillness of the night. Man did not concede. I saw the ensuing waves of gnats and flies with their ceaseless movement and incessant torment. Man did not yield. I witnessed as their own flesh rebelled against them. I watched as ice and fire filled the sky and locusts covered the ground. I saw darkness descend, and still, man's heart was hard.

Finally, I bore witness to the lost generation of Egypt in the stillness of a chilling dawn. They let Our people go.

Now that He had His people back, it was time to further develop the covenant He had made with Abraham. You see, the Father desired to commune with His people. His ultimate plan is expressly for that purpose, but the problem is His people, and all people, are impure and sinful. The impurity is brought on by their contact with death and the sin produced by their rebellion and evil actions. He is holy, and to be in His presence is to be in the presence of holiness. Sin and impurity are expelled from Him and cannot exist in or around Him. So, by His very nature, it would be impossible for mankind to ever speak with the Father without death being the result. So I was there as We talked together, Him and I, and He devised a plan. The plan would be to provide a cover over the impurity and sin; this would allow a communion. Although incomplete, it would be effective so He could speak with His people until the permanent solution could restore complete communion. It would require His people to walk a path of atonement. Only then could they see the differences between Him and them on justice, holiness, purity, mercy, and goodness. Only then could they strive and get close enough to desire a more complete relationship. Only then could they see and be aware of their sin and realize their need for a savior. Only then, after covering the foulness of their lives, could they desire for their hearts to be made pure. He made up His mind that He would be their God, and they would be His people. He decided He would live with them and speak with them.

So, as I walked with them from Egypt, Sinai, Paran, and Canaan—despite all the stubborn rebellion, backbiting, and complaining—I saw His heart and mercy unfold for Our people. I was there as the sea was split, as the pillar of fire lit the night, and as the cloud sheltered the day. I was there when manna rained down from heaven, and fresh quail was flown in. I was there as the ground swallowed up a people, as the bronze statue was formed, and as water sprang from a rock. I was there as the law came forth on the mount—as the hand of the Father etched ten simple commandments on tablets of stone. I was there as the plan was enacted, His path for atonement was shared, and the ark of His covenant with them was built.

I was there as Moses reasoned with Him. I enjoyed the relationship the Father shared with Moses. They talked with one another as friends. Moses was a humble man, and he coveted a closeness with the Lord that was unique, even among My prophets. Much like Elijah and Enoch, Moses is unique in his relationship with the Father. Sadly, Moses blurred the lines between savior and servant, and he missed the promised land. I was there as the stiff-necked, rebellious people tried the patience of the Father again and again. I was there when the evil report was given about the land that I had prepared for them, as the insurrection was kindled, and as the mercy of the Lord was lightly esteemed.

Before Moses passed from the earth, he relayed Our laws to the new generation with hope in his heart. His unrequited hope for a change of heart would rest until Jeremiah and Ezekiel could pick it up and carry it further. I was there when Moses breathed his last. Only two were found among that generation who could lead and believe—Joshua and Caleb. I was there as they, alone from their generation, took what the Father had prepared for them.

I was there as the Jordan River parted for My people. I was there as the prince of angel armies dictated that there is only one side—Our side. I was there as obedience and trust begot a great victory at Jericho, and when disobedience and disdain led to a momentary defeat at Ai. I was there at Mount Ebal and Mount Gerizim as the blessings and curses of the law were spoken into the world. I listened as the law was read. I watched as the blessings and the curses reverberated throughout the world from that place.

I was there as the sun stood still, as the victories piled up, as the immoral way of life was removed, and as the land was claimed and divided among Our people. I listened as Joshua expressed the same sentiments Moses did—to obey and trust in the Father, and all would be well; but behave as the Canaanites did, and be exiled as they were. There is one side, God's side, though the people did not heed Him.

I was there in the promised land, even when My people forgot me. They would forsake the Way, feel the desolation of their foul decisions, and then repent. We would save them and raise up and empower one to push back their oppressors. Yet they would again repeat the cycle. I was there as We upheld Our covenant with each judge.

I defeated the king of Mesopotamia with Othniel. I guided the hand of Ehud against the Moabites. With My strength, Shamgar brought down six hundred Philistines. It was My wisdom that defanged Sisera. It was Me they were signaling as Gideon and the three hundred blew the trumpets and smashed the clay pots. I showed the power of redemption through Jephthah in deliverance against the Ammonites, and it was Me that tore down the Philistine temple through Samson. I revealed to the people the miraculous in the mundane and the heroic in the humble. And still, the people would not listen.

In a time when My people should have been examples to the world, they became examples of the world.

I was there when, amidst the tumult of shifting loyalties and fading memories, a simple story of unwavering loyalty caught My eye. Ruth, a Moabite widow, clung to her mother-in-law, Naomi, and chose My people as her own. Through her steadfastness and loyalty, I honored her by making her one of My people—and even My earthly ancestor. It was a reminder that even in the chaos of societal decline, true faith could forge a path of redemption. But as time marched on, My people continued their cycle of disobedience and repentance, ever testing the bounds of Our covenant.

I was there when they clamored for a king like the nations around them, forsaking the unique position afforded to them. They preferred the sovereignty of man over the sovereignty of God, rejecting Me as their King. I was there as Samuel communed with Us over this sad affair. Still, the Father, in His mercy, would never force His people to serve Him nor force them on the path that would be best for them, and reluctantly, He gave Samuel leave to anoint Saul as the first king of Israel.

So began the tumultuous reign of kings in the time of Israel, Judah, and Persian captivity.

I was there when Saul began his reign with dignity and a sense of duty. I watched as his greed and pride ate away at him until he blurred the lines of king and prophet. His authority was divinely given, not divine in and of itself.

So I would select another. As the Father looked throughout the land, we found a king in the most unlikely of places. Instead of a towering man of stature, we chose a young, freckled, redheaded shepherd boy of obscurity whose heart had no equal. It's never been the appearance of a man that has moved the Father, only the heart. David is special to Me, and his heart was after the Father's. I was there with David as the oil flowed from Samuel's horn, anointing David as the next king. I was there as David protected his flock from the bear and the lion. I witnessed My people cowering in fear, Saul hiding in his tent, and David protecting my flock from Goliath with his faith in the Father. I was with David in many victories. I was with him in the palace and while he was on the run. Through his triumphs and betrayals, I was with him. When he messed up, he always humbled himself and returned to the Father. He knew the path of honor, and many mighty works of honor were wrought through him and those close to him. It was not in food or drink that he gathered his strength, but in My company. He honored Us, loved Us, and was loyal to Us. The Father did not let this go unnoticed, and He decided to honor him in return. So the Father said that I would not only come through the line of Abraham and Judah, but also now through the line of David. Many were spared and were given mercy for David's sake.

I was there as David's heir, Solomon, found favor in the Father's sight by asking God not for glory, riches, and power, but for the ability to govern wisely. To honor David's son, and out of respect for Solomon's goal, I bore witness to the endowment of wisdom and prosperity on Israel to a magnitude that has never been seen before or since. I was there as the temple was built, and what a beautiful sight it was. Sadly, Solomon, for all the wisdom he possessed, found himself lacking the strength to follow through on what he knew— always thinking he could appease and find a solution. He accumulated many wives and, along with them, their false gods and idols. He began slave labor and political moves for the betterment of Israel, but these were not part of My way; thus, he invited disaster into the land.

Through the greed of his descendants, a great division would be made, and eventual exile and captivity would be a result. Yet, through the succession of kings—some good, many bad—I remained. Through the division of My people into two kingdoms—Israel in the north and Judah in the south—I persisted. I was there, raising up prophets.

I stood alongside Elijah, navigating the treacherous reigns of kings with him. As he valiantly confronted Ahab's vile religious practices, Jezebel's cunning wickedness, and Ahaziah's stubborn defiance, I remained his constant pillar of support, empowering him in the midst of chaos.

I was there when the rain ceased, and fire fell from heaven, consuming all in its path. I was there in Zarephath as I magnified the meager oil and flour of a widow, turning scarcity into sufficiency—mourning into joy. I was there when life flowed back into the widow's lifeless son, proving that even the sting of death could be undone. Elijah was special to Us. He recognized and knew Our ways and Our voice. He would not follow another. He proved this on Mount Horeb when he recognized My presence in the simple whisper—paying no heed to the extravagance of the spectacular.

When the time came for Elijah to leave earth, I waited for the chariot of fire to bring him to Me. As he ascended, the mantle of his anointing fell onto Elisha, his faithful apprentice.

So then I journeyed with Elisha, traversing the rugged landscapes of Israel. Through Jehoram's pride and Jehu's violence, the idolatry of Jehoahaz, and the compromises of Jehoash, I stood unwavering—My strength doubling in Elisha, not diminishing.

I was there, working through Elisha as the waters of the Jordan parted and the bitter waters at Jericho sweetened. I was there as the oil jug refused to empty, and a barren woman embraced motherhood. I ushered in the miracles of the Shunammite woman's son returning to life, toxic food being purified, and meager meals being multiplied into feasts. Through the voice of Elisha, I healed Naaman in the cleansing waters of the Jordan, disciplined Gehazi, and showed the world that even the smallest of concerns matters in My eyes—as demonstrated when the sunken iron axe floated back to the surface. I gave Elisha wisdom that thwarted enemy attacks. I stripped the Syrian army of their sight, and even at Elisha's passing, I revived the dead through his bones.

But the chronicle of My presence with prophets did not end there. My voice echoed through Joel in Judah, foretelling the mighty outpouring of the Holy Spirit. I journeyed with Jonah, from his fear of a tarnished reputation, to his redemption in the belly of a great fish, and finally to the mercy shown upon Nineveh.

I walked with Amos, emphasizing that true worship went beyond rituals and entered the realm of social responsibility.

Yet the constant succession of Israel's kings still had little concern for Me and My things. I related to the heart of one of My prophets at this time. Hosea relentlessly pursued his wayward wife—so, too, does the Father chase after His often-errant people. In the midst of heartbreak and betrayal, Hosea's life became a living testament to My enduring love, My readiness to forgive, and My yearning for reconciliation. Through every tear he shed and every plea he made, I echoed the divine heartache for a people who often looked elsewhere, yet the promise that love would always call them home.

Dreaming of the day we could fellowship as we were meant to, I painted the prophetic portrait of My coming into the world and the suffering servant that I would become through Isaiah. I hinted at My birthplace and a time of peace when I would establish My Kingdom through Micah.

I was in Nineveh with Nahum, witnessing the fiery proclamations of its impending downfall. I walked alongside Zephaniah in Judah, echoing his urgent calls for repentance amidst the waywardness of King Josiah's reign. Together, we mourned the sins of the people and dreamt of a pure, humble remnant who would seek refuge in Me. He was not alone in his sorrow.

I walked with Jeremiah, the weeping prophet, in the turbulent times of Josiah's successors. We saw the burning faith of King Josiah turn into the ashes of his successors' dishonor. Through it all, I was Jeremiah's comfort, channeling through him My promise of a New Covenant, a hope to hang on to amidst despair.

With Habakkuk, I reassured that even when justice seems delayed, it is never denied. I spoke of faith through his lips,

reminding My people that the righteous would live by it—
even in the face of adversity. The people would not listen. So,
with captivity imminent, I walked with Ezekiel. I was with
him even as the northern kingdom of Israel fell to the Assyr-
ians and the southern kingdom of Judah to the Babylonians.
Though Jerusalem was razed, the temple destroyed, and My
people carried off into exile, I did not leave them. It was
through Ezekiel, My priest-turned-prophet, that the voice of
the Father would ring out amongst the exiles that He, the
Father, is not confined to a temple—that He, God, is the God
of a people, and even when they are exiled from their land
and temple due to their failures, they are not exiled from their
God. I was there as this point was driven home when the
Father allowed Ezekiel to witness His very own throne.

Though in captivity, there were those who would stay
loyal to the Father. In the heart of Babylon, I found a faithful
servant in a man named Daniel. Amid the noise and distrac-
tions of a foreign land, his fidelity to Me remained unbroken.
From a young age, he chose to honor Me, which would set
the stage for his life and ultimately transform a kingdom.
His commitment to the Father was so firm that he'd rather
face a den of lions than cease his communion with Him. And
so he did, and yet, he did not travel into that den alone, for I
was with him. I shut the mouths of those lions. He alone was
not the only one I saw in Babylon, though—I also was with
Shadrach, Meshach, and Abednego—young men of unyield-
ing faith who chose fidelity over compromise, even at the

risk of a fiery death. As they were cast into the furnace, the fire raging seven times its usual strength, I resolved to join them in their trial.

The furious flames danced wildly around us in that place, yet we remained untouched. In the heart of the furnace, I was their Companion. The blistering heat became a gentle warmth, the murderous fire a comforting light, as we walked unbound within the furnace, the flames yielding to our presence. I did not hide My involvement from onlookers.

Even with the cities abuzz with My involvement with those who remained loyal to Me, still the people feuded and scarcely hoped. So I rose up Obadiah as he reconciled the feud between Israel and Edom, conveying a dual message of stern retribution and comforting reassurance, balancing the scales of justice while rekindling the flame of hope in My chosen people.

I was there as My people's captors changed when the Persians overthrew the Babylonians. It was during the Persian reign when My people were once again put under threat of annihilation. I used the voice of Esther to quell the evil plot at work, causing My people to survive until their eventual freedom could be realized.

Though they were free, now back in their homeland, My people were still in bondage. During the Babylonian captivity, My people were battered both physically and spiritually.

So the Father devised a twofold solution—a solution that would rebuild them both spiritually and physically.

So, as the dust of Babylonian captivity began to settle, I stirred the hearts of Ezra and Nehemiah. I was there as Jerusalem was rebuilt both spiritually and physically. I listened as My peoples' hearts yearned for My Word as forgotten melodies of My laws once again echoed in the streets of Jerusalem. With a trowel in one hand to build the wall and a sword in the other to fend off invaders, they worked tirelessly, facing down opposition and discouragement to reclaim what they'd lost. Through this colossal endeavor, I was not just restoring the city's fortifications, but mending the shattered dignity of My people. Jerusalem's renewed walls stood as a testament to the resilience of faith and the power of unified effort under the guidance of the Father.

In this period of restoration, Haggai and Zechariah had a role to play. I took note of Haggai's determination and allowed it to rekindle the complacent hearts of the returned exiles. I listened to the hope of Zechariah and let it catch fire in the hearts of My people for My coming was not afar off.

As the echoes of the Old Covenant began to fade, I spoke one last time through Malachi. Together, we confronted the spiritual apathy that had seeped into the hearts of My people. We challenged the corrupt priests, reinstated the forgotten tithes, and reminded the people of their covenant responsibilities. But above all, Malachi's words bore the promise of a coming day, a day marked by the rise of the Sun of Righteousness, who would bring healing and renewed hope to a world yearning for salvation. This promise, shimmering on the horizon, connected the old with the new, bridging the gap until My arrival in the flesh.

And yet, as the centuries passed, the true purpose of My laws and commands was lost in a thicket of tradition, ceremony, and man-made regulations. My people had become rigid and legalistic, more focused on maintaining outward appearances than nurturing a true, loving relationship with Me.

It was finally time for the culmination and fulfillment of all of the prophecies and covenants made with humanity. As the Father and I talked, He laid out for Me what would be required of Me in order to bring about the hope We'd shared since the Garden. I chose to lay aside all the weight, glory, authority, and power that I had as Divinity, and I became just like any other man. This may not seem like a big deal to you, but for Me, after being so intimately close to the Father all My life, laying down that proximity and connection to be able to walk as a human walks was a monumental moment. I would still be connected to the Father through faith and prayer; I would be able to experience, hear from, and enact His will on the earth, but it would be different. I did make the choice gladly—for you, for Him, and for us.

So I came into this world to save the world, born of a virgin. I would be about My Father's business and accomplish His will even at a young age. There were a great many things I did in My life on the earth, so much that the world itself couldn't contain the lasting effects of what was accomplished through the Word becoming flesh. I recount the gathering of My disciples and the meeting of faithful servants and followers.

I was there gathering Simon Peter, Andrew, James (son of Zebedee), John (brother of James), Philip, Bartholomew, Thomas, Matthew, James (son of Alphaeus), Thaddaeus, and Simon the Zealot.

Each one of these men would carry with them My words and My Spirit long after I was gone. They would be the first generation among many brothers and sisters who would bring the Father, Myself, and the Holy Spirit to the world. So, I would teach them the Truth, show them the Way, and demonstrate to them Life. I nurtured faith in them daily.

I would teach them as they walked with Me. I would show them how to walk and live as the Father intended. They would uncover the heart of the Father and My teachings through the parables. In the stories of the Prodigal Son, the Lost Sheep, and the Good Shepherd, they'd recognize the Father's relentless pursuit of His children, the joy over one repentant sinner, and the selfless love that defines Him. The parables of the Sower, the Mustard Seed, the Growing

Seed, and the Leaven would highlight the nurturing of faith, illustrating the exponential growth of the Kingdom and faith even from the humblest of beginnings.

From the Good Samaritan and the Unmerciful Servant, they would grasp the essence of mercy, realizing the command to love neighbors selflessly and forgive others as they have been forgiven. The parables of the Workers in the Vineyard, the Unjust Steward, and the Talents would underscore the Father's fairness and the expectation of faithful stewardship with the faith and resources entrusted by the Father.

The Pharisee and the Tax Collector, and the Two Sons would enlighten them on the virtues of humility, repentance, and obedience over lip service, while the Rich Fool, and the Rich Man and Lazarus would starkly highlight the transience of earthly wealth and the importance of compassion. The Wedding Feast, the Great Banquet, and the Ten Virgins would instill readiness to respond to the Father's invitation and the impending return of the Messiah.

The parables of the Hidden Treasure, the Pearl of Great Price, and the Lost Coin would depict the invaluable Kingdom of Heaven, so precious that all else pales in comparison. The parables of the Wise and Foolish Builders, the New Wine in Old Wineskins, the Unworthy Servant, and Counting the Cost would offer lessons in practical wisdom, the transformative power of the Gospel, humility, and the cost of discipleship.

The Two Debtors, the Unjust Judge, the Persistent Widow, and the Friend at Midnight would illustrate the Father's gracious forgiveness, the importance of persistent prayer, and the Father's readiness to answer. Finally, the parables of the Weeds, the Net of Fish, the Budding Fig Tree, and the Barren Fig Tree would underscore the coexistence of good and evil, the final judgment, the discernment of times, and the expectation of spiritual fruitfulness.

I was there, every day, teaching and preparing them. Each parable, a gem of wisdom, would draw them closer to the Kingdom's values—justice, love, mercy, faith, and grace—enriching their walk with the Father and guiding their journey on earth. Through these parables, they would learn to embody the essence of the Father's Kingdom in their lives.

I was there, gently guiding them, teaching them to perceive the world as I did, to listen to the rhythms of a human's heart as I did, and to walk life's path in the way I demonstrated. I became their Compass, guiding them toward the essence of real repentance, as seen through the actions of Zacchaeus. I showed them the depths of true generosity, reflected not in the wealth of a giver, but in the heart, like that of a widow who outgave the wealthy with her modest two mites.

Through the fig tree, I unveiled the harsh realities of hypocrisy and the divine authority that would someday be theirs. This tree, with its apparent fruitfulness, bore no fruit, a hollow facade that was repugnant to me. I condemned it, sending a clear message that true worth is not in the pretense, but in authentic being. Upon seeing the withered tree the next day, My disciples were awestruck. Peter, in his wonder, invited Me to share his amazement. But instead, I used it as an opportunity to teach them the raw power of faith that was available to them if they would but shed their doubt and believe. This lesson would be emphasized repeatedly.

One such demonstration happened while I walked on water to rejoin My disciples. Their fear was palpable as I neared the boat. Peter, never one to shy away, dared to step onto the water with Me. He walked on the water for a moment, but as I mentioned earlier, doubt crept in when he looked at the wind and the waves instead of Me. I was there, ready to catch him—letting them all know that even when doubt creeps in and you lose your footing, I am there to catch you. The example of love is often overlooked, and this, too, was a point that needed to be emphasized more than once.

Specifically, there was another stormy night when I was getting some sleep belowdecks. I was awakened amidst a tempestuous storm with fear, doubt, and disbelief from my panicked disciples. I calmed the storm and questioned why they were so full of doubt. The disappointment I felt was not due to their inability to quell the storm, but their mistaken belief that they could perish while I was on board with them. Perfect love removes all fear, and that day, they demonstrated that they were not fully convinced of My heart toward them.

Guided by love, I was sent on a mission, not only to instruct My disciples and equip them to spread the teachings to the world, but also to manifest God's love to all who would seek Him. My role was to stand as the first among many brethren at the dawn of the Church, showcasing that anyone who sought after the Kingdom would find their needs met.

I introduced Myself with this principle to some of My disciples. They were weary from a night of fruitless toiling. Trusting My words, they cast their nets once more. Their leap of faith was rewarded with a catch so abundant their nets began to break. I'd even let them know that I was with them always when, before I ascended, I repeated this miracle for them. As dawn broke, after a night without catching anything, I stood on the shore, unrecognized. I called out to them, suggesting from afar off that they cast their nets on the right side of the boat. To their surprise, they hauled in a huge catch of fish, yet the net held firm. Recognizing Me then, they understood this miraculous catch wasn't just about the fish, and they rejoiced greatly.

All who sought Me and My Kingdom would find their needs met.

I was there as five thousand were fed from a humble boy's lunch of five loaves and two fishes. It was not just a day of miracles, but a profound lesson in the Kingdom's principle: When you seek first the Kingdom, God will take care of what you have need of.

Again, this lesson would be repeated for the world to see when four thousand people were fed. Once more, we found ourselves surrounded by a famished crowd. Their commitment struck Me; they had been with Me for three days without sustenance. Inspired by compassion, I multiplied seven loaves and a few small fish, providing four thousand with a meal.

There was another day when needs were met, and many enjoyed the fruit of a simple request of faith. At the wedding in Cana, My mother was the first to identify a problem, seeing that the hosts were about to exhaust their supply of wine. Unnoticed by the guests and overlooked by the elated bride and groom, she confided in Me. I told her, "My hour has not yet come." Yet she requested My help anyway and instructed the servants to obey Me. The Father chose to honor her faith and request, so I told the servants to fill six stone jars with water, which miraculously transformed into wine as they served it. The master of the banquet, oblivious to the miracle, was delighted by the superior quality of the wine. Hearing the wedding aglow with excitement over the new wine felt like a subtle precursor to the new covenant about to unfold.

All who would seek Me would find Me. All who would come to Me and ask for help would find it. The Spirit of the Lord was upon Me because He anointed Me to preach the Gospel to the poor; He sent Me to heal the brokenhearted, to proclaim liberty to the captives and recovery of sight to the blind, to set at liberty those who are oppressed. And I did just that.

I was there when the leper approached Me on a dusty road. His eyes pleaded for a mercy that his voice could not muster. I was there as the roof dust sprinkled from above, accompanied by the hushed anticipation of the four friends lowering their paralyzed companion. I was there when Jairus, a ruler among men, fell to his knees before Me. His heart echoed with the terror only a parent can know. I was there, in the midst of the crowd, when a woman tormented by a chronic disease of the blood sought relief from years of suffering.

I was there when the widow of Nain walked the mournful path to bury her only son. I was there when ten lepers stood at a distance, their voices carrying the weight of their affliction. I was there when the tranquility of teaching in the Capernaum synagogue was pierced by the screams of a man with an unclean spirit. I was there when a man blind from birth sat by the wayside, his world cloaked in perpetual darkness. I was there at the tomb of a dear friend, Lazarus, where his sisters wept, their hearts heavy with grief. I was there when a Roman centurion of great faith approached Me with a humility that contrasted his position. He felt such concern for his servant. I was there when the persistent calls of Bartimaeus, a blind beggar, beckoned Me for help despite the rebukes of the crowd.

I was there when, by the shores of Galilee, a man possessed by demons approached. His eyes reflected a soul shattered by torment, longing for relief. I was there when a deaf and mute man was brought before Me in the region of the Decapolis. His world was one of silence, his voice trapped within him. I was there when an official came to Me in Capernaum, his heart heavy with worry for his gravely ill son.

I was there when a man with a shriveled hand stood before Me in the synagogue, his limb a constant reminder of his ailment. I was there when a demon-possessed boy was brought to Me, the joy of his youth robbed from him by the tormentor within. I was there at the pool of Bethesda when a man who had been an invalid for thirty-eight years hoped beyond hope for a change to his grim state. I was there when two blind men followed Me into a house, their hearts echoing with the cry that was unwilling to go another day without sight.

I was there when a persistent Canaanite woman of great faith approached Me, pleading for her demon-possessed daughter's healing. I was there when a man, deaf and hardly able to speak, was brought before Me. He could not hear the sound of his loved one's voice. I was there when a woman crippled for eighteen years was in the synagogue, bent over, unable to straighten herself.

I was there bearing witness to a man possessed by a legion of demons who lived among the tombs, tormented and outcast. I was there when Malchus, the servant of the high priest, had his ear cut off in the Garden of Gethsemane. I was there when a mute man, imprisoned in his own body by a malevolent spirit, was brought to Me in Galilee. I was there when a desperate father brought his son to Me — the boy was tormented by a spirit that often cast him into fire and water. The father's faith was shaken, wavering on the edge of despair. I sympathized with his anguish and saw his desire for his son's deliverance.

I, the Healer, was there. So, what do you think happened in each of these situations? As faith and hope met love and grace? Each affliction, each torment, was replaced with wellness and peace. Not one left empty-handed.

In each of these moments, My heart was moved with compassion, love, and a desire to see them set free from their suffering. I was there as grace and faith wove a mighty tale of restoration, putting on display the Father's love.

There was one particular miracle that still had yet to be performed — a miracle that would change humanity forever, a miracle that would require a great sacrifice, a miracle that would put the love and power of God on display for all to see.

I remember pushing the weights and concerns of what was required of Me off onto the Father until We could discuss it. In the meantime, I sat down to eat supper with

My disciples. I felt it was time to share with them what was going to transpire. We communed with each other as I broke bread and drank to explain what was about to take place. I didn't even leave out who was going to betray Me.

Whenever it was finally time in the evening, I gathered My strength and laid My concerns before My Father in prayer. My body was under extreme stress and pressure because I knew the horror that awaited Me. It wasn't the physical pain of what was going to be done to Me—that is a very simple matter. The real issue was this: it would be the first and only time in all time and eternity that I would ever be separated from My Father. I knew what was at stake, though I loved you enough to follow through, taking your place.

Still, as I prayed to the Father, I knew how loving, infinitely intelligent, and wise He is. If there was another way you could have received salvation without Me being separated from Him, then He would have known it and done it, regardless of how difficult it might have been, because of His great love and desire not to be separated from Me. So, I asked Him for just that, knowing that if this was the only way, I was willing to do it—for you and for Him.

Upon leaving the Garden of Gethsemane, I understood that the path set before Me by My Father was not an easy one.

I was led before Pontius Pilate, Rome's governor, while the crowd called for the release of Barabbas—a known insurrectionist. The public chose him over Me—the Savior they had long awaited. This, too, was part of the divine plan. As they released Barabbas from his chains, they put Me in Mine.

They scourged Me—thirty-nine lashes delivered with brutal precision. Each one was a mark of the sins of mankind, each welt a testament to the sickness that gripped the world. Every blow was taken willingly, knowing I was paying the price for the redemption of all.

Shouldering the heavy cross, the rough wood biting into My flesh, I began My slow, agonizing march toward Calvary. The crown of thorns was pressed into My head, each spike a searing reminder of the mockery they made of My mission. Yet I pressed on, carrying not only the cross, but also the weight of the world's transgressions.

The sound of hammers driving nails into My hands and feet echoed through the air, each strike resonating with the pain of humanity's alienation from the Father. Suspended between heaven and earth, I bore the agony and the scorn, the taunts of those who did not understand. As they gambled for My clothes, I remained steadfast, My thoughts on you, on all of mankind, and on My Father's love, which guided Me even in My darkest hour. My thoughts were interrupted as I heard a voice coming from beside Me. It was a thief asking for My remembrance as I entered into My Kingdom. He hoped in Me, and he is with Me still in heaven.

When the time had finally come, I gave up My life, and I descended into the depths of hell. For three days, I waged a battle there, a battle for the very keys of death and hades that Adam had relinquished so long ago. It was there that I confronted the darkness, the ultimate price for humanity's freedom.

But My Father's plan was not for Me to remain there. After three days, He called Me forth from the abyss, the power of His love stronger than the chains of death. It was then that I rose, triumphant and alive, forever changing the course of history, paving the way for mankind to be reunited with its Creator, its Father.

I woke within the tomb, My body wrapped in linen cloths, the scent of myrrh and aloe heavy in the cool air. The pain was gone.

There, in the soft, gray light of the morning, I met Mary Magdalene. She wept, grief clouding her vision. At first, she did not recognize Me. Mistaking Me for the gardener, she pleaded for information about My body. I said only her name, and then she recognized Me. I told her not to cling to Me, for I had not yet ascended to the Father. I asked her to go to My brothers and tell them, "I am ascending to My Father and your Father, to My God and your God."

With the dawn of My resurrection, a heavenly mandate was bestowed upon Me. I ascended to My Father, carrying with Me the redemptive offering, the price of humanity's sin.

As I approached the mercy seat, I did not present the blood of goats or calves, but My own, shed for many. As the High Priest of a new covenant, I laid My blood at the mercy seat, fulfilling the righteous requirement of the law. The veil was torn, the old covenant had been fulfilled, and the new had begun. Through My offering, the way was open for all to approach the Father.

Then, back on earth, I appeared to two disciples on the road to Emmaus. They were leaving Jerusalem, hearts heavy with sorrow over My death. Their eyes were kept from recognizing Me initially, and so I explained the Scriptures to them, beginning with Moses and all the Prophets, interpreting to them in all the Scriptures the things concerning Myself. Their hearts burned within them as they listened, their despair slowly replaced with hope. It was only when we broke bread together that their eyes were opened, and they recognized Me.

Later in the evening, I appeared to My disciples, and I greeted them. They were quite joyful as they saw Me. I breathed on them, saying, "Receive the Holy Spirit. If you forgive the sins of any, they are forgiven them; if you withhold forgiveness from any, it is withheld."

A week later, I appeared again to the disciples; this time, Thomas was with them. He had doubted my resurrection, demanding physical proof. I gave him the proof he was looking for. I told him that there is a more blessed way to live, to have not seen Me and yet still believe. This is the essence of living by faith and not by sight, after all.

Later, I appeared by the Sea of Tiberias, revealing Myself to My disciples again. I performed another miracle, filling their nets with fish after they had caught nothing all night. We shared a meal together on the beach—bread and fish.

Then it was time to restore Peter. I took this time to speak with Peter. I asked him three times if he loved Me. Each time, he affirmed that he did.

My last meeting was with all eleven disciples on a mountain in Galilee. I gave them their Great Commission: "All authority in heaven and on earth has been given to Me. Go therefore and make disciples of all nations, baptizing them in the name of the Father and of the Son and of the Holy Spirit, teaching them to observe all that I have commanded you. And behold, I am with you always, to the end of the age."

After these forty days, it was time to return to My Father. I told them of the Holy Spirit and where they were to wait to receive Him. Finally, as I was blessing My disciples, I was carried up into heaven—where I now reside, making intercession for you.

Every promise that was made was made for you. You are the beneficiaries of the new covenant made. Instead of having a high priest talk to God, you can come talk to the Father directly, with Me as your High Priest. I walked the earth as you walked. I know what it is like to be tempted, to feel deeply, and to desire hopefully. Though I never sinned personally, as I took your place on the cross, I came to know the weight of sin and the guilt and shame that accompanies it when the sin of the entire world was placed upon Me.

Though My time with a physical body had concluded, My story is far from over. I was there, My friend, when the Holy Spirit descended into the upper room, carrying with Him the power and presence of the Father He had just been with an instant before, flooding that room like hurricane winds from heaven. The Church would be born on that day, with thousands to be added to its number daily. Many could see Me in My disciples who walked with Me on the earth. They spoke with authority, great deeds were done, the sick were healed, the oppressed were set free, and all their needs were met.

The Church would not be confined to those who had shared in My earthly journey, absorbing the wisdom of My words and witnessing the miracles of My actions. Instead, the Church would transcend such boundaries. The Church would be an earthly room in the Father's house, where My brothers and sisters could have a place to call home until they come home. It is a place where introductions can be made between you and Me—a place to start a relationship that will last an eternity—a place of power, provision, and hope—a place of joy, peace, and faith. It is no longer confined to an ark, a temple, or a mountain, but is now and for always in the hearts of My people. Wherever they gather, I am in their midst; whenever they call out to Me, I am there.

One young man, Saul, didn't walk with Me during My earthly journey. He'd come to be known as Paul, and he knew Me as you know Me. Each of My eleven disciples who walked with Me on the earth did mighty wonders and exploits for the glory of God, but so did Paul, and so can you. It was him that I'd have write thirteen letters to My beloved Church, writing a good portion of My New Testament.

You are all of the same generation. You are all members of My Church, citizens of My Kingdom, and part of My family. The apostle Paul is just as much your brother as somebody who walks with you today. Every Word in My Holy Word is just as alive today as the day it was written. It is incorruptible and everlasting. It is the source of strength and stability in the world. It is the guiding light, the channel of faith, and the breeder of hope. There is nothing that can temper its boldness, nor dull its impact. That Word was there at the beginning, that Word was with the Father, that Word became flesh, and that Word bore the sins of humanity, whipped Satan in hell, and returned triumphantly to reign over the joyful freedom the Father had long desired for those who would call Him Abba. I was that Word, I am that Word, and I will be that Word.

I was there at the birth of this world, the creation of man, the rebellion of man, as waters flooded the earth, as plots were made and covenants struck. I wept with the judges; I counseled the kings; I inspired the prophets. I was there in the rise and fall of kingdoms, in the battles won and lost, in the hopes and heartbreaks of a generation chosen and called by God. Through the faith, doubt, obedience, rebellion, triumph, and tragedy—I remained. And with every turn, I echoed the promise of a new covenant to come—one not written on tablets of stone, but on human hearts. It is your heart. The new covenant marks a new generation of God's people turned into God's children. A living temple to house His Spirit, vessels of honor set aside for His use, ambassadors to carry His Words with you wherever you go. I am here.

This epic tale of God and man, the Bible, this divine love story woven through the centuries, has been leading up to this pivotal moment. You see, in the beginning, the Father walked with Adam and Eve in the cool of the day, in perfect communion, in a beautiful garden. This was His initial design, to share life with us in an intimate, unbroken relationship. But when sin entered the world, that relationship was disrupted. A chasm was formed, separating mankind from their Creator. Yet, even in the midst of that separation, the promise of redemption and restoration was born. Since then, every word, every act, every covenant, and every prophecy has been a stepping-stone on a path designed by our heavenly Father, a path leading you back into His loving embrace.

You have seen love and redemption played out on a grand stage spanning centuries, with its climax at the death and resurrection of His beloved Son, Me. Just as I was there and even played a part Myself, it is now your turn to play your part. My challenge to you is to enjoy it.

I am here with you in every moment, every breath you draw. You are never alone. Reach out to Me, for I made a promise to My disciples—a promise that extends to you: I am with you always, to the end of the age. I am not confined to the annals of the past; I am near you, walking with you. I am your Shepherd, guiding you; your Friend, standing beside you; your Hope, uplifting you; your Way, leading you; and your Peace, calming your spirit.

In the days of My earthly ministry, constrained by a physical form, I was bound by place and time. My words were dispatched from a single location. But now, through the sanctifying power of the Holy Spirit, who has chosen you as His temple, we can commune freely. You can reach Me, and I you, at any hour of any day. The pivotal moment once expressed is this: The intimacy once enjoyed by Adam in his walks with the Father in the Garden can be yours.

The Father has demonstrated His immense love, mercy, and grace in an epic narrative, bringing you to where you stand today. He desires to share the deepest parts of your life, to journey with you as you explore, dream, and discover the grandeur of His creation and the gifts He has bestowed upon you.

I have given you My name, an emblem of My authority. In My name, you shall bring light into darkness, free those ensnared by fear, heal the sick, restore sight to the blind, and spread the good news of the Gospel. I am no longer tethered to human form, and the Spirit of the Lord is no longer simply upon humanity, but within it. You carry My authority, not as a burden, but as an honor, and with it, the mighty power of the Holy Spirit. You are more than a passive recipient of divine grace. You are an active agent of My love in this world, a vessel of My power, a torchbearer of My light. Stand firm, for you are endowed with a divine purpose.

You are not an accident in the grand design. You are intentional, a masterpiece carefully and lovingly created in Our image. Our Father, like a Divine Potter, delicately and intricately shaped you with wisdom and with purpose. You bear My mark, a testament to My love and My promise.

Never doubt your worth in Our eyes. The price We paid for you is beyond compare. This is the measure of your value to Me. You are not simply loved; you are so profoundly loved that I gave up everything to ensure you could stand beside Me. I am the Friend who sticks closer than a brother. I am the Shepherd who leaves the ninety-nine to find the one. I am your Fortress, your Deliverer, your Shield.

Let My love be the compass that guides you, My Word the light that illuminates your path. Let My peace guard your heart and My joy be your strength. For you are Mine, a precious child of the King—a warrior of light in a world of shadows, a bearer of truth in an age of deception, a vessel of love in a sea of indifference.

So, go forth with courage, knowing you are never alone. Live out your faith boldly, for you carry the Kingdom within you. Let your life be a testimony of My grace, an echo of My love, and a reflection of My glory. I am with you, always, until the end of the age and beyond.

I was there, I am here, and I will be there.

I am coming back.

In the grand tapestry of time, a day approaches, a day etched in divine promise, the day of My Second Coming. I shall descend from the heavens with a shout, accompanied by the heavenly symphony of the trumpet of God. The dead in Christ shall rise first, bursting forth from their earthly tombs, reborn in glorified bodies, shining brightly with immortality.

Following this miraculous resurrection, those who live, those who kept their lamps burning in anticipation of My return, will be transformed in the twinkling of an eye— their mortal bodies transfigured into the splendor of eternal life. Together, we will ascend to meet in midair, a reunion of heavenly proportions, where we will remain with the Lord forever.

The adversary will rise in a final, desperate gambit. A beast, emblematic of false authority and counterfeit power, will appear, wielding influence over the inhabitants of the earth, attempting to lead them astray. The adversary will present illusions of peace and prosperity, demanding fealty, enforcing his mark as a symbol of subservience. But know this—those who choose this path abandon their place in the Kingdom of Heaven.

And yet, in the face of this escalating deceit and oppression, I will not stand idle. I will send My two witnesses, clothed in sackcloth, to prophesy and proclaim the truth— their words a beacon of light in a world shrouded in darkness. They will wield divine power, casting judgments and displaying signs, revealing the lies of the adversary.

Then, the climactic battle of Armageddon will take place. The adversary, in his hubris, will rally his forces in a futile defiance against the Kingdom of God. I will return, not as the Suffering Servant, but as the Victorious King. With a sharp sword from My mouth, I will strike down the nations, and the adversary will be bound, his reign of deceit and destruction brought to an end.

This, however, is not the conclusion of our shared journey. On the contrary, it is but the prologue to a glorious age. I shall return to earth, not as a sacrificial Lamb, but as a reigning King. With righteousness as My scepter, I will establish a thousand-year reign of peace and justice, the likes of which the world has never seen.

During this millennium of tranquility, the lion will lie down with the lamb, swords will be beaten into plowshares, and humanity will learn war no more. Tears shall be wiped from every eye, death and sorrow will lose their sting, and love will prevail over all.

But even after these thousand years, our story will not end—for I will then usher in a new heaven and a new earth, where righteousness will dwell. No more will there be a sun to govern the day, nor a moon the night, for God's glory will illuminate all, and I, the Lamb, will be its lamp. The gates of the holy city will never shut, for there will be no night, and the nations will walk by its light.

In this new reality, every tear will be dried, and death will be but a faded memory. Mourning, crying, and pain will be relics of the past, for I will make all things new. In the heart of the city will be the tree of life, bearing twelve kinds of fruit, and leaves for the healing of the nations.

So, My friends, the best is yet to come! Until then, I love you and look forward to our next chat.

Jesus

About the Author

Jake Provance is a Christian who is also a writer. With the help and direction of the Lord, Jake has written twelve books with sales totaling in the millions. Jake is a graduate of Domata Bible School in Tulsa, Oklahoma, and he has a call on his life to minister the Gospel however the Lord directs him. Jake is a husband to Leah; a father to his son, Elias; son to Keith and Megan; brother to Garrett and Ryan; and ultimately, a child of the Most High.

Feel free to connect with him at:
Jake@WordAndSpiritPublishing.com

Other Inspirational Books by Jake Provance

Keep Calm & Trust God - Volume 1

Keep Calm & Trust God - Volume 2

Keep Calm

(hardback gift edition - includes volumes 1 & 2)

Let Not Your Heart Be Troubled

Scriptural Prayers for Victorious Living

I Am What the Bible Says I Am

I Have What the Bible Says I Have

I Can Do What the Bible Says I Can Do

Jesus Is King

Keep Calm Devotional Journal

You may contact Jake at
Jake@WordAndSpiritPublishing.com